BY DAVE ARTWOOD

C✚DA
BOOKS LTD

CODA
BOOKS LTD

www.codabooks.com

This edition is published in Great Britain in 2012 by

Coda Books Ltd., Office Suite 2, Shrieves Walk, 39 Sheep Street, Stratford-upon-Avon, Warwickshire CV37 6GJ

www.codbooks.com

Copyright © 2012 by Coda Books Ltd.

All rights reserved. No part of this publication may be reproduced or transmitted in any form or by any means, electronic or mechanical, including photocopy, recording, or any information storage and retrieval system, without permission in writing from the publisher.

Photographs courtesy of Pictorial Press.

A CIP catalogue record for this book is available from the British Library.

ISBN: 978-1-78158-198-8

CONTENTS

CHAPTER 1 4

CHAPTER 2 18

CHAPTER 3 43

CHAPTER 4 54

CHAPTER 5 69

TRACK-BY-TRACK ANALYSIS 80

CHAPTER 1

IRON MAIDEN are much, much more than just a heavy metal band... In 1970, the United Kingdom laid claim to the world's first heavy metal act in Birmingham's Black Sabbath. The history of that band deserves its own chronicle, but suffice it to say that this small and sceptr'd isle has gained much self-esteem from the pioneering work of Sabbath – if, that is, you don't take into account their patchy output after their lead singer Ozzy Osbourne left them in 1979. For a while, the future of British metal looked dodgy, to say the least, with only Judas Priest and Motörhead left to fly the flag. However, the smiles were put back on Brit-metal fans' faces with a vengeance when we invented heavy metal for the second time with the NWOBHM, or New Wave Of British Heavy Metal. As Sabbath sank into mediocrity and other titans of heavy music such as Led Zeppelin and Deep Purple reached their sell-by dates, a new sound was required – and one duly emerged with enormous power and impact that same year, spearheaded by the state-of-the-art music of Iron Maiden. A deeply melodic, dexterous sense of musicianship wedded to aggressive riffs straight from the Sabbath early catalogue, Maiden's early work was a blast of fresh air in the dank, stagnant atmosphere of late-70s metal, itself also under threat from the nascent punk movement.

Along with future stars such as Def Leppard and Saxon and less successful (but still incredibly influential) NWOBHM bands such as Diamond Head and Blitzkrieg, Maiden drew the rock-consuming world's attentions back to Britain – where, with the honorable exceptions of the USA, Germany and Scandinavia, they have remained focused ever since. Now do you see why Iron Maiden aren't just a metal band?

The road to glory goes back as far as 1975, when bassist Steve Harris was playing in a band called Smiler. Although Harris was a fan of many musical styles of the day – from prog-rockers such as Uriah Heep and Yes through to glam acts such as The Sweet – he found himself increasingly dissatisfied with his bandmates, who didn't see much merit in the self-penned songs he presented to them. At Christmas that year he left Smiler, intending to form a new act in order to perform original material with a musically aggressive edge. The name he chose for the brand-new band was taken from a film of The Man In The Iron Mask which he saw at this time – thus putting paid to the rumour that the name Iron Maiden was a reference to the Prime Minister at the time, Margaret Thatcher, despite her nickname and the fact that she appeared on early Maiden single covers…

Harris later explained of the band's inception: "I didn't start the band as any kind of crusade against punk, as people seem to think… I couldn't have because Maiden began in 1975, before all that, doing East End pubs like The Ruskin Arms in East Ham and The Bridge House in Canning Town. It was when Zep and Purple were finishing – a lot of the influences came from them, the twin guitars from Wishbone Ash and Thin Lizzy, the time changes from Yes and Jethro Tull. We wanted to get all the ingredients in there and come up with something different. But after a year or so we realised we weren't getting gigs any more… Then we did hate punk. We felt pissed off that these guys just picked up a guitar, jumped around a bit and, because of this so-called 'energy', they got the publicity and they got the work. But they couldn't play and we could – though I know that sounds big-headed… I went to The Roxy once because we were offered a gig there and I'll never forget it because there were geezers spitting all over each other! Well, we had quite a hardcore following and we knew if we went down there it'd all be off, ructions."

Steve borrowed £3000 from his aunt to keep the band going, as Murray told Q later. The bassist added: "We had to be well organised. We started doing our own T-shirts, a couple of hundred at a time. The kids liked them because they were like an 'Up yours' to the people who put metal down all the time. We travelled all over the country to get gigs, Aberdeen and Blackpool over a weekend and back to work on Monday. We fixed up this big old Austin van we called the Green Goddess with space for the gear and nine bunks in the back for the band and the crew – who were mates, we couldn't pay them. We'd sleep outside the gig and wake up in the morning with frost on the blankets... We had smoke machines, bubble machines, all home-made – bung a bit of dry ice in an electric kettle, that sort of thing. Then a singer we had, Dennis Wilcock, started us thinking. He had this stunt where he waved this sword about, then slashed the blade across his mouth and blood would come pouring out. Of course, it wasn't real, but a couple of girls did faint right in front of him once – the Stars And Stripes Club, Ramsgate, I'll never forget it. Still, he looked a bit daft, to be honest. So we came up with the first Eddie the 'Ead, this horrible mask which stood at the back of the stage. We rigged up this pump we got out of a fish tank and at a given moment it would spit buckets of blood all over the drummer."

Where Maiden immediately stood out was in their adaptation of the speed and attitude of the punk scene, while retaining the musically experimental edge of the prog-rock dinosaurs and even some fusion sensibilities thanks to the pioneering songwriting of Harris and the skills of the early line-ups, although musicians came and went with surprising frequency. Taking their cue from bands as diverse as Queen, Led Zeppelin, Wishbone Ash (whose distinctive twin-guitar sound rapidly evolved in Maiden's early work), and Judas Priest, Maiden quickly honed a set of steadfast set classics which have stood the test of time to this day, three decades and more later.

Playing regular gigs on their home turf of London's East End, Maiden endured constant personnel shuffles before a stable line-up coalesced. The first singer, Paul Day, was fired for a lack of charisma, while his successor Dennis Wilcock – who covered himself in make-up and fake blood on stage – took things too far the other way, although he did recruit a guitar-playing friend called Dave Murray into the band before his departure. This irked the extant guitarists – Dave Sullivan and Terry Rance – to the point where Harris was obliged to split the band for a short time, although Maiden subsequently reformed with Murray as the only guitarist. Another axeman, Bob Sawyer, was let go after causing friction between Murray and Wilcock – obliging Harris to fire both men, a surprising revelation for anyone familiar with the former's subsequent long tenure in the band. It got worse: a single gig in November 1977 with Tony Moore

on keyboards, Terry Wrapram on guitar, and drummer Barry Purkis (who later renamed himself Thunderstick for a job in Samson), led to Harris sacking the whole band.

However, Harris was not keen to give up so easily and brought Murray back, as well as a new drummer, Doug Sampson, and a new frontman named Paul Di'Anno. The latter gave the band a new edge, with his punk-influenced look and sound: he would front the band for their first significant taste of success. The new line-up – Di'Anno, Harris, Murray and Sampson – then recorded a demo, the now-legendary The Soundhouse Tapes. This 1978 demo featured three songs and sold out its run of 5000 copies in a matter of weeks, most of which were snapped up by the rabid East End following that the band had amassed in previous months.

As Steve told writer John Stix: "'Prowler' is a very special song for us. When we made The Soundhouse Tapes we took the actual tape to Neal Kay who was a DJ in north London. He used to have a heavy metal chart which was compiled from record requests and printed in the music magazine Sounds. 'Prowler' got to be number one just from the requests for the demo tape. That's why we had the tape made into a record, because so many kids were asking us how they could get hold of the demo tapes... The Soundhouse Tapes were the very first thing we recorded. It was just a demo. It only cost us about $400 to make the whole thing. It really wasn't great quality."

Of The Soundhouse Tapes, Murray said: "Well, that was [financed] between two guys in the band, really. We were working at the time, doing day jobs. We were always putting money back into the band, as far as getting equipment and petrol. You gotta pay to play nowadays. You always had to, really, especially in the early days. So, we just self-financed it really... We couldn't actually afford to buy the master tapes, which would have been nice tohave now. We just scraped up enough money to do the recording. But, to actually buy the reel of tape would've cost more and we couldn't afford that. So, unfortunately that's gone… They just re-recorded over it, the next band that goes in. Unfortunately, it's gone to magnetic heaven… we only had 5000 made up, and gave a lot of them away. It was more of a promotion thing really. I gather they're very hard to get hold of and are going for $300-$400."

Championed by the heavy metal DJ Neal Kay, Maiden hit the top of Sounds magazine's Heavy Metal Soundhouse chart with the song 'Prowler', as well as scoring two songs ('Sanctuary' and 'Wrathchild') on the seminal 1980 NWOBHM compilation Metal For Muthas. It wasn't long before Steve's amazing bass technique was noted by the musicians' community. He later said of this: "I do get a lot of people saying that I've influenced them, which obviously is very flattering. But, the truth is, I'm really more interested in trying to write great songs. Maybe it's because I'm a bass player and I write a lot of the music. I grew up listening to a lot of different bass players like Chris Squire and John Entwistle. Also, Martin Turner from Wishbone Ash and Rinus Gerritsen from Golden Earring were both a very big influence on me. If you listen to some early Golden Earring records, you can really hear the influence!"

He said of his playing style: "I play a lot of bass chords and stuff. I'm not too analytical about my own playing, I just write the songs. I'm more concerned with what's good for the song than with what I'm playing. Which is probably why I've been playing less of a role lately, because that's the way the songwriting has been. That's what's needed. The songwriting always depends on what's needed or not needed."

Of his writing style, Harris explained: "Some [songs] I write with a main bass riff and work out the melody on top of it. Some songs begin with a strong melody line and I work out the music behind it. I pretty much work everything out on the bass, the actual riffs and the harmonies. 'Running Free' came together when I put a riff to the main drum beat by Doug Sampson."

Maiden appeared not to take the NWOBHM tag too seriously, with future singer Bruce Dickinson commenting later: "It's not a movement. It was almost as if in 1977, suddenly from nowhere like spontaneous generation, all these bands suddenly appeared like locusts. And it isn't like that at all. There have always been heavy metal bands. There are still as many up-and-coming HM bands in England as there ever were, when Iron Maiden and Samson and Saxon and all those bands came up. The difference is there just aren't as many record companies interested or prepared to take the new wave tag because record companies had a pretty easy time with New Wave. All they had to do was make records cheaply – because the bands in most cases couldn't play too good, and really didn't care about playing much anyway – stick them in the back of a Transit and send them off to Sweden, and that was New Wave. All very anarchistic and revolutionary... But unfortunately a lot of

record companies went round signing heavy rock acts in exactly the same way, just throwing shit at the wall and hoping some of it sticks. Because it actually does cost a certain amount of money to support a heavy rock band on the road, because they tend to do things slightly different to a new wave band. A lot of bands – not us – just wanted to get an album out because they were convinced, no matter what the record company was like, they could set the world on fire."

Steve's down-to-earth attitude has always propelled the band, not least when he is asked about the band's future: "You can't really say what's going to happen. I take each month or whatever as it comes. Y'know, I just want to play for as long as possible onstage. I want to go to different countries and play to different audiences. So basically I'm having a good time at the moment and I want to have a good time for as long as possible, and I don't want to think about the day when I'm going to have to think about something else… It is similar to a football

thing. You know that at 32 you're going to have to give it up... Y'know, I don't really regret that I didn't make it as a footballer. I couldn't really be dedicated to it. Because when I went round to West Ham, my favourite team, it's all I ever wanted to play for, and when I got down there I found that it wasn't really what I thought it was. You know what I mean? I didn't want to go to bed at ten o'clock in the evening. I was at that age when I wanted to go out and have a few beers and meet a few women and that."

Of the old NWOBHM days, Steve recalled to Shockwaves: "There was a bit of a buzz about us at the time. There were actually a few companies who came out to see us; in fact, I think we got turned down by CBS and A&M. Even though we were playing pubs at the time, we had all these fans from the East London area who would follow us around all over the place. When we would play in East London, none of the record companies would come out to see us, they only hung out in central and West London. East London was like the wilderness, so they would never venture over there... Motörhead were already fairly well received by that time and were headlining venues. We actually did a couple of support gigs with them. We weren't really aware of this movement that was happening until the press started getting hold of it. There were bands up North like Saxon, in Yorkshire, and there was Witchfynde, as well. So, there were all these bands happening all over England during that same time and I don't think anyone was really aware of it until the press started writing about it, and that pretty much started that whole movement."

After handling all guitar duties for almost two years, Murray was joined by a sequence of temporary axemen, starting with Paul Cairns in 1979. Of songwriting and guitar playing, Murray once advised: "Don't try and play a million notes. Playing one or two notes with feeling is a lot better than going crazy sometimes, you know? I think, as well, just play with melody. I've done the same thing, when I first started playing I'd sit down and listen to stuff and I'd nick ideas, but the more you're playing the more you're developing your own kind of style, so I think if you play for fun and enjoy yourself... you make an album and you kind of listen to it and play it over and over, then you tend to let it go and you move onto the next thing. If we're going to be doing a song for a tour that we haven't played for many years, you have to sit down and re-learn it. It comes back because it comes there subconsciously, but you have to sit there and re-learn some of those notes again, but it happens once or twice and I think it's a good thing actually... we're proud of everything we've done in the past and when we do an album we want to put 150% into it, so when you listen to an album a few years back and think, oh yeah that sounds good, then you know you must've been doing the right thing at that time."

Dennis Stratton was more successful, recruited despite the band wanting to hire Murray's friend Adrian Smith instead (however, Smith had his own band, Urchin, at the time). At this point Sampson was also replaced by Clive Burr, who was introduced into Maiden by Stratton. All this activity led to a major coup in December 1979 when they signed a deal with EMI, assisted by the efforts of their new manager, Rod Smallwood (who they laughingly nicknamed 'Smallwallet' for his penny-pinching ways). The fanbase, which had grown thanks to the scintillating shows Maiden performed (aided by a stage mascot called Eddie, whose face was based on a decaying death-mask seen in a picture of the Vietnam War) and rejoiced in the deal with EMI.

Of the recording process, Dave Murray once explained: "We go in there and it's kind of like a football team or something. You all plan together, you want to make it work or whatever, and you want to work on the details and I think that's what's

important. We work on the small stuff as well as the big stuff... then you've got Bruce singing, you've got all the melody and stuff, it's just making a lot of musical statements by Maiden. There's a lot of depth to Maiden and it's the sort of [music] that is probably going to take you a few times to listen to it to really get into it, so there's a lot going on. I think it's great because you can play it over and over and you'll hear different things every time you play it, there will be more stuff you didn't hear the first time round."

To many observers' surprise, the eponymous debut album went all the way to No. 4 in the UK, despite heavy metal's supposedly lowly stance when ranged against the likes of new wave and disco. This rise to glory did not go unnoticed by the elite of journalism, who often seemed keen to see Maiden fail. Asked by Sylvie Simmons at Creem if the band had lost its edge, Bruce retorted: "I don't think we have, and I don't think we ever will lose it, as long as we keep on with the same attitude which we've had, which is: go out and go for it. That's what got us the cult following, in the same way that I think AC/DC went out and got that cult following with Bon Scott. Because when you went to see an AC/DC show, whatever else you got, you always got 100 percent from the band. And you always got lots of blood and lots of sweat and everything, and that's what you still get if you go to see an Iron Maiden show... If you go in with the attitude that the thing is just a job, then of course it will become a job, and you go onstage with all the inspiration of a plumber's mate, or something like that."

After the band had built up a reputation for their huge shows, there was no turning back, as the singer said: "There really wasn't any alternative, because there was no way we were going to pick up radio airplay. We do now – but that's because of the touring. We haven't changed our style to fit American radio; American radio has come to us and said, we feel we've got to play you because when we open the phone lines for requests, all we get is abuse because we're not playing Iron Maiden. They don't really want to play the band, but they've got to, because there's so many people they can't ignore it. I think that's a very healthy situation…

"See, press and people like that in general misunderstood the whole thing that is heavy rock. They don't comprehend the extent of the dedication of not only the band themselves, but usually the fans that go with the band. To them, pop music means disposable music which sells disposable articles. As far as we're concerned, our music isn't disposable music which sells disposable articles. As far as we're concerned, our music isn't disposable, it isn't designed to sell anything, and all we ask is that people listen to it and enjoy it…

"This is something I've been doing since I was 13 years old, since I first listened to Deep Purple In Rock – that was the record that got me involved in rock music, full stop. And ever since that age, I've been involved in some way – for the first three or four years listening to it, and then getting around to trying to play something. It's not like I suddenly discovered something new in my life – 'aha! A cause! A movement!' It's always been part of my life, and I think heavy rock is part of a lot of people's lives. Because everything is getting more disposable and more plastic and more throwaway every second. In that way we're a bit of an anachronism, really."

CHAPTER 2

BY 1980 the New Wave Of Heavy Metal was a recognised phenomenon in the press and the boardroom alike, with record companies snapping up Maiden's contemporaries in an effort to emulate their money-generating success. The band themselves made history by touring the USA in support of Kiss, who at the time were enjoying critical adulation with their Unmasked tour after a couple of years in the doldrums. Further dates in support of Judas Priest saw the band's profile elevated still further, unhindered by the replacement of Stratton with Smith, who had been the target for recruitment all along. The Smith and Murray guitar recipe was the key to the early Maiden sound, alongside Harris' penetrating fingerstyle bass and Di'Anno's semi-melodic, semi-staccato bark.

Of the music itself, Bruce mused: "The intensity that people put into music has been the same since the year dot. There's no dilution of intensity in what we do. There's the same kind of intensity in what we do as there would have been in the music some medieval lute player did in the court of King Ned. He really gets into it and everyone goes, yeah! What a raving lute player! Y'know, and he smashes his lute up at the end of every gig or something. That kind of intensity has always attracted people and galvanised them. It's an intensity that there is in heavy metal and yet it's always fucking clobbered. Nothing else is clobbered like heavy metal... I would describe our music as being anything but bland. You put an Iron Maiden album on the turntables and watch your fucking mother-in-law drop the dishes or something. It's not bland at all; it sticks out like a sore thumb."

Steve explained of the subject matter: "Well, we don't deal with all the experiences that we have in life, we don't sing about everything that we go through. There's lots of different things that I'm into that I don't particularly want to write about. I'm into football, but I don't want to write a song about it. I might one day, if I get the inspiration to write about football, y'know, or about anything. A lot of it is a fantasy thing. Y'know what I mean? People get a bit fed up with having politics rammed down their throats... people have said to us, y'know, you're a working class band, why don't you write about where you come from? And about politics and that, and how hard done by you were and all that business, but y'know, we don't want to... all the films that are successful at the moment are talking of the unknown things that people don't quite know about. Like 666 and all that, that's just one song, there are other songs that deal with reincarnation and things, y'know."

The second album – 1981's Killers – was another step forward, with the band mostly eschewing the punk stylings of the debut

for a more polished approach that saw the beginnings of Harris' career-long penchant for long, epic songs. The tour that followed it was characterised by the band's relatively debauched offstage antics, although – unlike many acts of their age, ilk and era – they never indulged much in drugs, preferring a few pints to the ubiquitous cocaine of the day. Nonetheless, Di'Anno took it too far, drinking too much and becoming unreliable as a result. With his vocals and performances suffering to unacceptable levels, Harris asked him to leave.

At the end of 1981 Di'Anno's replacement was drafted in. Bruce Dickinson, then as now a key mover on the British metal scene, was completely different to his predecessor. His voice was a spiralling, über-melodic thing of beauty – inspiring literally hundreds of power metal vocalists in the following decade – and he was an educated product of the middle class, literate and articulate in a way that Di'Anno had never been.

Dickinson had attended a public school, Oundle, near Northampton, saying: "That was a classic case of parents wanting their kids to have everything they never had... Some of it was good, loads to do, amateur dramatics, debating, but really it was the most illiberal place on the planet. Wacko! Mass floggings over minor practical jokes. Eventually I was expelled for pissing in the headmaster's dinner. Somebody informed on me. It was only half a cupful slipped into the frozen beans, and I knew from biology a bit of boiled urine wouldn't do him any harm. Ill-judged, though, I admit".

Dickinson brought the right influences to Maiden, as he said: "I'm still a Ritchie Blackmore fan. I love watching the guy. I think he's miles away from what he was doing in Deep Purple, but then that's understandable because that was 12 years ago and the guy gets older and wants to move on and do different things. I remember when I was 14 or 15, that one particular album, Made In Japan, made a really profound impression on me. Really profound. I used to just sit and listen to it over and over again. I used to know the whole thing note perfect – every drum beat, everything. Like the first couple of Sabbath albums, and Jethro Tull's Aqualung, and Arthur Brown, would you believe – great... My favourite bands all come from the '69-'75 period really; not a lot after that. But really, it's not so much whether it's new or old, it's the quality. In the old days bands were less prepared to compromise – that's not true actually, plenty of bands compromised, but bands that didn't always ended up being our firm favourites. Bands like Purple. It's that attitude, I think, that inspired me to get into rock music. And unless I see that sort of magic coming from a band when you see it live, then I'm not really interested, no matter how pro or note-perfect. If somebody has got inside your head and motivated you, you go away thinking, now let's go and rip off whatever they did!"

He added: "I still read Biggles books – it's great, picturing yourself in the cockpit, big scarf sticking out and everything. It's fun... there is a slightly more serious side, but everything is treated with a certain amount of humour. Within the band we do have a strong sense of humour about what we do, although we do take it seriously. I think there's a lot of humour in life, and I think that's fairly accurately represented. We have a very black sense of humour, hence the album covers. We watch Halloween and Poltergeist and things like that."

As he told the NME in 1988, his musical education started at the beginning of the 70s: "The first Black Sabbath album had come out and there were a lot of very heavy art-rock bands about, playing the kind of music that Wagner might have played. I'd just got hold of a copy of Deep Purple In Rock and Aqualung, so there didn't seem to be any alternative. Pop was really crass at that time, all the Bay City Rollers stuff, and jazz rock was very boring, everyone going booooooooing on bass... Then there was

T. Rex and Bowie and I couldn't stand either of them. I don't like the singing; I couldn't stand singers who whined. I remember hearing 'All The Young Dudes'. I could never stand Mott The Hoople... I was into the blues but I wasn't infatuated the way Led Zeppelin were. I always thought Led Zeppelin were terribly overrated, like Jimi Hendrix, who made a few revolutionary tracks and a lot of shit. Deep Purple was what really moved me. I'd never heard a band play with so much power, so loose and yet so ballsy... I wanted to be a drummer, not a singer. If it was a case of choosing between John Bonham, who went biff, bang, wallop or Ian Paice, who did thirty million drum rolls to a second, I wanted to be like Ian Paice. I ended up being a singer by accident. Basically I couldn't afford a drum kit... Anyway, I decided I wanted a group with the lyrics of Van Der Graaf, the playing and proficiency of Purple and the energy of punk. It was a pretty tall order for a bunch of university students, jumping around like punks, playing like Ritchie Blackmore and writing songs like Jethro Tull, but we had a shot at it."

This willingness to experiment with multiple styles would come to the fore in his lyrics, which explored new territory on later albums. Interestingly in retrospect, it emerged that the respected radio DJ Tommy Vance – whose judgement was usually spot-on in all other areas – advised Bruce not to join, reasoning that his band Samson had a greater chance of success. Fortunately for band and fanbase, Dickinson ignored him and went on to sing on 1982's fantastic The Number Of The Beast, a step up on all levels.

When NOTB was released, its frankly terrifying cover art – a pièce de résistance from the band's long-time sleeve artist of choice, Derek Riggs – identified it and its creators as one of the most important metal phenomena ever. The lead single, 'Run To The Hills', was a huge hit, as was the album itself, which entered the Top 10 of many countries despite rightwing pressure

groups in America protesting against the supposedly 'Satanic' music and art. Fuel was added to the fire by tales such as that of producer Martin Birch, who damaged his car in a crash and was presented with a bill for – wait for it – £666.

Asked by Paul Morley of the NME in 1982 if the image of the band was as important as the music itself, Dickinson mused: "I think you could be right. I think there is more to the actual music side than that. As far as the overall image goes, the way Eddie is related to Iron Maiden, there may be a lot of truth in what you say. Oh, sure, he's definitely larger than life, but in other ways he's very much tongue-in-cheek. He's not to be taken deadly serious. People can find some fucking serious grief about Eddie, saying that he's real horrible, but it's no way that it's anything other than a good laugh… There's a lot of humour about us, put it that way. We try and debunk a lot of your standard heavy rock poses. We do a bit of it ourselves but at the same time we take the piss out of it… because we're human beings and we don't take the whole of life completely, stupidly seriously, and all we want to get over is that we're just normal guys out for a good time. I think that the music stands up on its own, but there is no reason why you shouldn't give a show that is a good laugh… I suppose [fans] want to see people who can play, they respect certain values like professionalism, and they don't want to be treated like shit. They pay good money and they look forward to seeing some good music being played by decent musicians who really put their soul into it. If a pile of shit walks on, well, they'll soon let you know if they don't like it. You can't get away with just farting."

And so Maiden entered their period of greatest commercial power, going on to release four albums which both defined and evolved 1980s heavy metal. 1983's Piece Of Mind was the first, featuring the talents of ex-Trust drummer Nicko McBrain, who had replaced Burr.

Unlike many drummers, Nicko avoided using double bass drum pedals, saying: "I find that using one is hard enough and I think that using two would be double trouble! ...it depends on what the bass line is laying down. The more intense it is, the more you have to play on the foot. It just comes from a lot of playing. One of the most important things to be aware of is your balance. By this I mean how you sit behind the kit in relation to the distance from the bass drum and the height from the floor. I sit very low and my upper leg is parallel to the floor. I only use the side of my big toe on the bass drum pedal. You should find what works best for you."

Nicko explained: "My father played the trumpet and keyboard and my mum was into the piano, so there was always a heavy musical element in my house growing up. I was 11 years old when I saw Joe Morello play a solo with his band in 1964. I knew straight away that that was what I wanted to do. My family was totally supportive... I'm self taught. But I learnt from the best drummers in the world by listening to what they played and took in as much as possible from them."

Of the many fans of his drumming, McBrain opined: "I wouldn't say that I'm proud, it's more of an honour. It is very nice to know that people appreciate my playing. When I was a young boy I always wanted to do the best that I could and I guess that that means, that when you have a passion for something, you give it all and you will eventually meet your dreams."

Powerslave followed, including all-time Maiden classics such as '2 Minutes To Midnight', 'Aces High' and 'Rime Of The Ancient Mariner'. With Dickinson and Harris – then as now the primary songwriters – exploring metal-friendly themes of warfare and fantasy literature, the albums were bought in their millions worldwide, and seized upon equally by fans in many countries, especially those where Maiden put on their electrifying shows. The latter element of the Maiden experience was encapsulated in 1985's double live album Live After Death (all metal fans have to have that poster on their wall!) and a more experimental, sci-fi focused album in 1986's Somewhere In Time. Not that Maiden had an entirely free hand: wanting to record a song on the subject of the famous science-fiction novel Dune (and to include a spoken-word excerpt from it), Maiden received a refusal from the author Frank Herbert's agent which ran: "Frank Herbert doesn't like rock bands, particularly heavy rock bands, and especially rock bands like Iron Maiden".

Murray told writer Gary James of a recent record-label switch: "I don't really know the politics that goes down between the management and the record company. We get on with the music and let them deal with the business side of it. CMC is a really good label. They're really looking after the band. They're really into it. They're very enthusiastic. You need somebody that's gonna be behind you, and be a team, and we're playing on the same team. They're an independent label, but they're really pushing the band, and also releasing the back catalogue. Now everything we've ever recorded is on CMC. They've got everything we've ever actually put down on tape. They feel good about having us with them and we feel vice versa."

Various concerned parents' groups still warned of the dangers of listening to Maiden, of course. However, Maiden later mocked the idiotic Satanic controversy by including a 'sinister' reversed message on the song 'Still Life', which – when played backwards – was revealed to be McBrain doing an impression of Idi Amin, saying "Hmm, hmmm, what ho, sed de t'ing wid de t'ree bonce. Don't meddle wid t'ings you don't understand" ("What ho, said the monster with the three heads, don't meddle with things you don't understand"), followed by a burp.

"I think it's pathetic," said Bruce to Creem. "Water off a duck's back, really. It was fun to play along with it a little bit last year, because the album was called Number Of The Beast, and they seemed perfectly willing to give us oodles and oodles of cheap publicity. But I'm just fed up with it now. It's boring, it's tired, and I think even the Moral Majority's getting fed up with it. You don't need to play up to that sort of publicity. We're quite capable of going out and entertaining people live without having to go out and seek cheap publicity... Journalists are journalists because they write words better than they write music, so consequently they don't understand that the reading of rock lyrics is not reading poetry. Rock lyrics are designed to be sung. I mean, 'wopbopa loobop a lop bam boom, got a girl named Daisy who's driving me crazy' – it sounds great when Little Richard is singing it, doesn't it, know what I mean? So I don't think you can really knock lyrics. If the cap fits, wear it. The bottom line is if they sound OK when they're sung. I will admit that there are a couple of lines on this album that we thought were real funny at the time, but we kept them in because we didn't want to go through the grief of arguing about it. So we kept them in and we all go 'oooooofff!'

Of his entry into the band, Dickinson explained: "When I first joined Iron Maiden it was already locked into a Grand Guignol style, which mainly comes from Steve and these traumatic nightmares he had. He never tells anyone about them, he doesn't like to go into it, but obviously that's why a lot of his songs follow those themes. Though not so much any more I don't think, I gather he has a slightly more peaceful night's sleep these days. Over the years he's done 60 to 70 per cent of the lyrics, the rest are mine, and that's about the mix between shock-horror and other topics... What I do is the big melodramatic bit, mock-opera style – opera with razor blades. You can get away with those lyrics that way, it doesn't sound too crazy. Mind you, once in a while I have said, come on, you've gotta be joking! I remember once he came along and said, here's one: 'In a time when dinosaurs walked the earth / In a land where swamps and

caves were home' – all this to a merry Irish jig rhythm with these octave leaps in the middle. I thought, bloody hell! But I did it more to prove it could be done than anything else."

Of the use of new sounds, Murray explained, "We'd use anything, if it sounds good we'd use it. It just seems having the orchestration and using the keyboards and synths to do that it just makes it sound bigger and fatter and gives a more dynamic sound to it all, but if you strip everything away, the songs are strong enough to stand out by themselves. You just want to enhance a piece of music and make it sound the best it can sound, so if you want to use keys to add a particular effect to a song, I think it's good! To me there are no rules in music, if it sounds good to your ear and if it sounds good musically, you can use a set of bagpipes if you want, whatever makes that song sound its best..."

The new, slightly experimental approach of Somewhere In Time – which had featured keyboards and guitar synths – had obviously not put off the Maiden fanbase, so the band took the approach a step further on what is regarded by some as the finest

(if also most commercial) album of their career to date, Seventh Son Of A Seventh Son. A concept album about a child with second sight who must steer clear of hellfire and other unpleasant fates, the record was supported by a triumphant performance at 1988's Castle Donington festival (although the show itself was marred by the deaths of two fans, crushed during an earlier set by Guns N' Roses). In 1990's Guinness Book Of Records the show was cited as the loudest gig ever played.

It was a mighty show. "I'm an entertainer," said Bruce once. "I feel more like some sort of bizarre juggler... We're just there to see that it reaches a climax at the right moment. Ceremony as a release is used all over the place, whether it's formal or informal. A football match is a ceremony of release. The key is to defuse it, so that people can tell the difference between the ritual and reality. The ritual releases feelings that, if put into practice in the modern world, would end up killing them. Songs like '2 Minutes To Midnight' are about that bit inside you that actually wants to be in a gunship in 'Nam, hosing down all those gooks... Some thrash metal bands seem to have a bit of a problem with it, but I assume it's tongue-in-cheek, as I've met them, and they're the most mild-mannered people around. I don't think the imagery is such a problem. I mean gory imagery for sensationalism's sake has been around for a long time, back as far as Grand Guignol theatre and stuff like that... when the music gets disruptive and dangerous, the only people it's usually dangerous for is the audience. Joe Soap can get onstage and say 'Let's trash this place dudes!' but he's not the one who's gonna get his head caved in and spend the night in a cell."

Of the intense stage show, Bruce once explained: "It's like you're building yourself up all day and then just letting it all go during that two hours. You have to visualise what's happening... I shut my eyes and think of the people in the audience and it's like a huge sea and the waves come rolling over you and you're part of it, and it's like you're part of this huge great thing... you can call me an old fucking hippy, I don't care. The whole thing is just absolutely great. I suppose it's like a meditation and it's like when I'm singing and there are no distractions, there's a little voice that you become aware of that's singing along with you and you're aware of the crowd..."

Occasionally gigs got a bit too violent. Of one gig in Paris, Bruce told Q in 1991: "Moshing is dangerous and it really pisses me off... There were 15 people down the front absolutely hell-bent on beating the crap out of anyone who didn't want to join in. I'm talking about huge skinheads hurling themselves at whoever's in the way, boy or girl. People were getting hurt. My whole thing with rock, especially heavy metal, is that despite the musical aggression, the feeling is always of comradeship, people looking after one another, because you're all into the same bands and it doesn't matter whether you're rich or poor, thick or Brain of Britain. This moshing thing is really egocentric and it screws the show up for everybody."

With the end of the 1980s, Maiden fell into something of a critical and commercial rut from which it took them years to recover. Perhaps the large-scale desertion by metal fans to the new grunge and alt.rock scenes in the early 1990s had something to do with it, or maybe the band's records just sounded a little old hat in the new, self-aware era of plaid shirts and angst: whatever the cause, something about Maiden just sounded a little out of touch in the new decade. This wasn't helped by the departure of Smith to his own band, ASAP: he was replaced by Janick Gers of Gillan, who to this day is not quite the fan favourite that each member of the classic Dickinson/Murray/Smith/Harris/McBrain was in the 1980s, even though his musical skills have never been in doubt. Of his departure, Adrian said: "I had begun to get tired, bored, and really didn't know what I wanted to do. I enjoy it more now, because I used to have no personal life.

Balance is necessary, something that we didn't have back then. When it is time for us to work, we are all revitalised because we have the opportunity, outside of Iron Maiden, to follow our personal choices."

Janick Gers had a distinguished past, explaining: "I got a phone call from [since-disgraced paedophile] Jonathan King who assembled [the band Gogmagog] around 1985. He liked my blues style kind of playing and thought that I would give them a good slack, and that's what he thought it would mean, and... He wanted me to join the band with Neil Murray, Clive Burr, Paul Di'Anno and Pete Willis who used to play with Def Leppard. So we got together and we did a session which we recorded and we put it out and it was quite a good fun thing actually... [Then Ian Gillan] rang me up one day and asked me to drive to London. I went to the Top Of The Pops studio and... Bernie Tormé had just left the band, so I went down. I didn't know any of the songs beforehand. I only knew that I would be playing at Top Of The Pops and everything was new for me. The guys just told me basically: 'Learn these songs for tomorrow'... so I went into my room and suddenly the tape ran out while I was learning them. Next day I said to them: 'Sorry guys, I haven't learnt the songs, my tape was running out...' And when we got on the stage, we did a one-hour sound check which was me learning the songs. And that was it. I personally think I played good enough that night, though... I played with Deep Purple a couple of months ago. I did a jam session together with them and that was great! I really like [Gillan]. He's still a great singer. He, Plant and Paul Rodgers... they wrote the book of singing some time ago, you knew that?"

Gers and Dickinson went back a long way, as the former explained: "I met Bruce when I was in White Spirit. Bruce was in a private school and I was in a public school. My old band White Spirit and Samson were often playing in the same kind of places. We both came from the same genres and we had the same kind of backgrounds... I was playing football with [sometime Marillion singer] Fish and [Bruce] asked me to come to the gig to watch him, and he ran me out and said he was looking for a player and I said OK. So, I got that gig and Bruce was doing that same gig as well and we met again in a few years and... Basically we hadn't seen each other in a long time. I was recording a Bowie track 'All the Young Dudes'. Tony Hadley from Spandau Ballet was originally supposed to sing the song, but he got sick at the last minute, so Bruce sang it. That's how we got together. The rest is pretty much history..."

1990's No Prayer For The Dying saw Maiden return to an older, rawer style, moving away from the experimentation of the Seventh Son era – but to less critical acclaim than they could perhaps have expected. However, No Prayer... did yield the band's only UK chart-topping single to date in 'Bring Your Daughter To The Slaughter'.

Further line-up problems lay ahead; however, this time with Dickinson, whose desire for a solo career had never been hidden from band or fans. Releasing a solo record and touring with Gers in his band, he returned to Maiden for 1992's Fear Of The Dark, which performed even less well than its predecessor.

Bruce announced while on tour that he would be leaving at its end, leading to some slightly bizarre vibes within the camp. Dickinson's departure caused a few ructions, as revealed by Kerrang! magazine in 1993 when they published an interview with a slightly inebriated McBrain: "He's going his way, we're going ours. Fuck 'im – let's get a new singer! That's it... cut'n'dried... My father, rest his soul, said to me once: 'Son, if anyone ever shits on the McBrain name, they'll only do it the one time'... He's said, 'Fuck you, I'm off'. If that ain't shitting on you, then what the fuck is? I told Steve what my old man said, and I think he thought it was a sensible analogy! It seems to have been a culmination of things for Bruce. He's been writing screenplays, books... He's got his fencing and his family. It could have been pressure from his wife, for all I know. He hasn't said anything, but it's a possibility. Plus, he went to LA, and y'know what the fucking wankers are like out there! 'Oh, fuckin' Bruce Dickinson, you awesome motherfucker, duuude! Yeah, you'll make a great fuckin' career on your own! Leave that bunch of fuckin' has-beens behind!'... [I] love the geezer – I've worked with him for 10 years. I'll always be there for him, but I still feel hurt, 'cos I know he don't like the band any more. At this stage, that ain't fuckin' cool... Some nights, I see Bruce sing like he hasn't sung before. Tonight wasn't one of them. Sometimes I can't hear him, and wonder whether me monitors are fucked! He's skylarking about – that's OK, that's the way he deals with it. But I eat, live, breathe and shit this band. And I do feel that he don't really wanna be here. Everyone's felt a little of the same about Bruce's effort, and how he's performing. But we mustn't let it get to us. We've got so much strength from each other, and from the whole fucking deal, that it's bonded us together. To me, this is still a Fear Of The Dark tour. It's not a Farewell To Bruce tour. It's got fuck-all to do with that. What I feel, although in a positive way rather than a hateful one, is good fucking riddance! I can't wait to get to the end of this tour and find a new singer. He and I have done interviews together, where I've said stuff like, 'I'm gonna take him outside and fucking do 'im!' It's a laugh, but there's also an element of truth in that! In my heart of hearts, I don't want to be doing this. I want us to find a new singer and do a new album. There's still a good fucking bit of mileage left in this band. We ain't dead yet. Where there's a will, there's a fucking way. It's gonna work for us; I know it will. Everyone's so positive... It's like the phoenix rising. We will rise again, as a stronger and more positive bird..."

Dickinson himself, from the centre of the commotion he was causing, told the same reporter: "[The tour is] very strange, really. But I don't get the sense that it's anything other than a really enjoyable experience. This is certainly a lot easier than the other way of leaving Maiden, which would've been to sit there, gnashing my teeth and dumping it on the band after the tour's over. This way, it's out in the open. And all I see in the audience is people smiling. It's like they're saying, 'Bye... It's been great!' That's that!... I've had no hate mail or death threats, either! In fact, I've been knocked out by how broad-minded people have been... Experienced Maiden-watchers were probably geared up to have me disappear two or three years ago, around the time of Tattooed Millionaire [Dickinson's first solo LP]. At the end of this tour's first chunk, I was due to make another solo record, and looking back at the whole Fear Of The Dark thing, it hadn't quite worked out as I thought it might. I still think it's the best album we did since Powerslave, but I also think I've been creatively sleepwalking for the last five years. The rest of the

band and all the fans love being locked in the straight, narrow direction that is Maiden, and there's nothing wrong with that. But I kept trying to deviate from the rut, saying, 'Look what's up here, guys!' I just ended up drained. I realised that I was trying to drag this huge thing somewhere it didn't wanna go!"

Bruce added that some slight friction had always existed in the band: "There was much more friction between '81 and '83 than there ever was afterwards! We nearly came to blows on the Number Of The Beast tour. In fact, Steve wanted to fuckin' sack me after two weeks, but Rod [Smallwood, Maiden manager] said he had to live with me! Steve isn't a guy who naturally likes change. He's conservative with a small "c" – very quiet and reserved offstage. He's very determined about keeping control of Maiden, and maintaining its direction. All that early tension between us actually fuelled the band! But towards the end, there was this little something inside of me, screaming 'For God's sake – there must be something different that you can do!' Some nights on the last leg, I'd think to myself, 'Why does this feel so much like hard work?' You then start to realise that... actually, perhaps... you don't want to do this any more... [The band] will probably become very much more Steve's baby now, and I certainly don't think it'll plummet just because I've gone. Iron Maiden is like an old warhorse. The Trooper, the charging Roy of The Rovers, the straight arrow, the ball at the back of the net... that's what Steve is. From a personal point of view, I wouldn't like to see Maiden play Guildford Hall. I think that would be very sad. But then again, if people are happy doing that, it's OK!"

Dickinson said of Steve: "We haven't really had that many conversations over the last 10 years! He's not really the kind of bloke you could sit down with in a pub and pour your heart out to! He's more of a "pass the salt" sort of chap. We have different approaches to feelings. He keeps all his locked up, and I'm in the process of trying to splatter mine all over my music. I would have liked to splatter more emotion over Iron Maiden's music. But it doesn't work. It's not the kind of music you can do that with! [The lyrical imagery] was quite intriguing, 'cos no-one was doing it. But after a while, all the allegorical stuff I tried to slip in became so tenuous. I started to think, 'Why don't you just say what you mean?' If I'd had my way, Maiden would have expressed more feelings and opinions, from the very beginning. Steve has always felt that it's dangerous to over-analyse things, and most of his songs are about fear… I actually think this is an opportunity for them to grab it by the balls, and change. They obviously don't see it that way!"

Of the final tour, Harris said: "Bruce is really only doing this because it's already been arranged. I know he wants to go out on a high note and all the rest of it, but I also know he'd rather have left beforehand. Maiden aren't going to split up. We were obviously disappointed at Bruce's timing, but the situation's known now, and we can find someone else. Bruce definitely jumped, rather than being pushed. I was surprised, because he seemed totally into the Fear Of The Dark tour's first leg. I was actually the last one to know, because I was out in Florida, mixing the live album. They didn't wanna tell me, 'cos they knew it'd do my 'ead in! The reaction was disappointment, sadness, being pissed off... all at once! But we've all felt that he's been doing so many different things, that something had to give eventually. The thing is that if he can't give Maiden 100 per cent, then we don't want him in the band! That's no disrespect or animosity, but there's no point in persuading him to come back or anything. In fact, if he back-tracked now and said he wanted to stay, we probably wouldn't let him! Personally, I think he's maybe made a mistake, 'cos I don't see why he couldn't do his solo thing and Maiden. But I suppose he wants to do other things too, and Maiden are a hard-working band… It's weird having someone on stage that's going. Very odd. Both sides, if you wanna split up like that, wanna get on with their own things. At the moment, it's in limbo, but we're still doing really good gigs. It really pissed me off when someone suggested that we've only announced Bruce's departure 'cos the tickets aren't doing well! That's a fuckin' insult – we'd never do that... I believe we'll carry on and be as good as ever. If I didn't believe that, I would stop... Me and Bruce don't 'not' get on. I like and respect him, and I like to think he feels the same, but I wouldn't say we're great mates. But that's not to say we won't go and have dinner at each other's houses... but there's no point in getting too upset. You can't keep people on a ball and chain. Some bloke in Spain was saying, 'I want to kill Bruce – he's a traitor!' but that's ridiculous! To be completely honest, this hit me at a time when I was at a bit of a low ebb anyway. But you have to pick yourself up and steam back in. That's the way I handle things... I think it's the only way I know how. When Bruce has problems, he doesn't really let 'em out. I think I like to talk about problems more than he does... I suppose sometimes we don't want to bother

each other with our personal stuff in this band, 'cos there's so much chaos on the road as it is. A lot of personal stuff I've been through in the last year, with my divorce and stuff, leaves you at a low ebb. Anything else that goes wrong really gives you a kick in the teeth... What worried me was that I've always felt confident about Maiden. Bruce quitting knocked me for six, and I thought maybe the rest of 'em would be looking to me to be a leader. For a week or so, I didn't feel like that, but now I feel stronger as time goes on..."

CHAPTER 3

BRUCE DULY left the band and Maiden were plunged into an era from which many feared they would never emerge – the Blaze Bayley years. Blaze was the singer in the UK Britrock C-league band Wolfsbane, and although he had a perfectly decent set of vocal cords, he found it hard to step into the considerable boots of Dickinson, who was by now enjoying a profitable solo career as well as flying planes and writing comic novels. Of Wolfsbane, Bayley recalled: "We did three albums with Def America and two with Bronze Records. I was actually in a band before that, called Child's Play, which kind of had a Thin Lizzy vibe. With Wolfsbane... we had been royally fucked so many times making the compromises we had to make, especially after the first album.

"The record company or management would always have their way, yet they would blame us if the record didn't do well or if the show wasn't well received. The few times that we did stick it out and manage to get it our way, it was successful. We were broke the whole time as well, which didn't help. But I'm very proud of the records I did with Wolfsbane."

Fans never really accepted Bayley, although he recorded two competent Maiden albums – The X Factor in 1995 and Virtual XI three years later. Although sales of both were adequate at best, Maiden – and their manager Rod Smallwood's new record company Sanctuary, by extension – kept things afloat with lucrative tours and the release of two compilations, A Real Live One and (oh, stop it) A Real Dead One.

Harris told Hard Force magazine in 1993 of Fear Of The Dark: "We really enjoyed the Fear Of The Dark tour much more than any other tour... We are really looking forward to touring

again and playing gigs in towns that we couldn't visit last year. Our huge enjoyment is obvious on the two live albums, and we're very pleased with them. The energy of the band on stage is perfectly rendered. There really was this little extra something during the last tour... this is the first Maiden album that really reflects the personality of the band. On the previous albums, we used to hide our ideas behind allegorical terms, or we'd use mythology and legends: this was somehow masking our real feelings as human beings. This time, we show these feelings and this gave our music another dimension... we never found a standard musical formula... It simply doesn't exist, and we evolve with every album. This isn't an abrupt change, but something more progressive, and we do believe that we are changing. We are becoming more straightforward and we aren't afraid to express our feelings."

Always a football-loving band, Maiden had incorporated their obsession into the new album, telling Shockwaves: "Well, this is our eleventh studio album and over the last couple years in particular, more and more young kids are getting into soccer, not so much here, but in the rest of the world, people are soccer mad! Especially in places like Italy, Spain, and South America. We headlined the Monsters Of Rock festival on our last tour and when we played Sao Paulo, I would wear Brazil's soccer shirt, and when we were in Argentina we would wear the Argentina jersey. The fans over there give us loads of shirts because they know how much we're into soccer, and the fans get so into it. So, we thought it would be great if we could tie the two together... it's our eleventh album, the World Cup is coming up, and we're totally into soccer. So to tie in with Virtual XI, we have the five members of the band and the 11 is made up of six international soccer players. It's great fun, and it's brilliant for me because of my love for soccer."

A computer game called Ed Hunter was unsuccessful at this

point, despite Blaze's support for it before its release: "Iron Maiden was planning on doing a video game for a long time, but with this band, we always want everything to be the best quality and the best representation we can have for our fans. The technology didn't really exist to do justice for an Iron Maiden fan until now. We were approached by a company in England, and they had a few ideas and a couple of the guys who were working there were actually huge fans of the band, so they had a really good handle straight away of what an Iron Maiden game should be about, featuring Eddie. We had some meetings with them and I had a real strong idea for the story where each album cover is a level of the game. So, the first couple albums is in the streets, which we turned into a whole virtual environment so you can walk around the streets and encounter all the different characters. And the Powerslave cover we turned into a whole 3D environment where you can walk into the pyramids, and you also get to go into the future and enter the torture chamber and the X Factor. The album covers are brought to life into a 3D environment and Eddie is a 100,000 [pixel] hologram character, which is more than the T-Rex in Jurassic Park. The game is titled Ed Hunter because you're hunting down Eddie. The idea is, the heads of the five members of the band have been chopped off and you gotta go and find them! At the same time, you're trying to survive Eddie, because he's trying to stop you from getting to the next level."

The multimedia effort went into overdrive at this point, with the writer Mick Wall compiling an official Maiden book at this point. As Steve said: "We actually had an official book released around the Somewhere In Time era, but this new book is basically about everyone in the band, and people who have worked with the band, from its conception up until now. It's quite interesting, really, even for me, because of the different viewpoints. When I edited it, I basically left things as is, even the things I didn't necessarily agree with; I think it's important for people to have their viewpoints. The only things I really changed were any errors in technical points that were slightly wrong... I haven't seen Dennis [Stratton] for a long time, and Clive [Burr] I saw about four or five years ago. But some of the other guys, even Doug Sampson, the original drummer, I still see him. And our first guitar players: Dave Sullivan and Terry Rance, I still keep in touch with them."

A compilation titled The Best Of The Beast kept fans' interest high at this time, as did a bonus track recorded specially for it. As Blaze explained: "I think what also makes this album quite different is the fact that we recorded The X Factor for quite a long time and did a whole world tour. We took a little break in the middle and recorded a track called 'Virus' for The Best Of The Beast. And that gave us a lot more confidence when we started writing for this album. I had learned so much about the different areas of my voice and I made it stronger. I feel that the recording of this new album was also a lot more spontaneous than the last. We just got the arrangements together and started

recording before we even rehearsed the songs."

Steve was now Maiden's de facto producer, as he explained: "I do enjoy it, but it's a lot of hard work. I suppose I kind of co-produced the earlier albums, and arranged the songs. In a way, I'm very glad I worked with Martin Birch on the previous albums because I learned a lot from it. I also mixed the two live albums, A Real Live One and A Real Dead One, because Martin decided to leave. So, I had to hire an engineer and, fortunately, I had some experience in the studio."

The inevitable occurred in 1999 when Bruce Dickinson returned to the band, alongside Smith, who played alongside Gers and Murray in an unprecedented three-axe line-up. Of the three-guitar set up, Murray told Undercover: "When we had the discussion, we never went into rehearsals to see if it was going to work, it was verbally done. Adrian's going to come back into the band at the same time as Bruce is going to come back into the band, and that was it, so we sat down and started putting the feel together for Brave New World, it was a very natural process.

"We sat down and worked out... you know, there's a lot of details to work on, but basically having three guitar players it really moulds together very well. It can sound like one big guitar or it can sound like three individual guitars. It depends what piece of music we're playing at the time, but we get on well together and it's a very natural environment, you know? There's different ways of playing things on a guitar, so we kind of do it so it moulds together and sounds like one unit if you like... There are a lot of slow passages, when you need that clean sound as well, so basically those amps are very versatile and also with the Fender Strats as well, they're very versatile guitars so all three of us use Strats anyway. We're like the old purists really, so it's like Strats and Marshalls, but we're using more of the clean stuff as well as the heavy stuff...

"We do a lot of harmony guitars and we do a lot of unisons, but it's kind of going back to our influences as well. A lot of bands like Thin Lizzy and Wishbone Ash used harmony guitars and we've taken that concept and added it into our own unique way of playing. With each song there may be a harmony guitar or unison, but it's basically whatever fits the song, we just like to take full advantage of it. Hey, you've got three guitars, so it's just doing as much as you can, you know? Also it's a thing where you want to complement that particular song, we wouldn't just do it just for the sake of doing it, it's there just to enhance a particular melody or [add] a musical statement to that piece of music... with three guitars we can do three guitar part harmonies, which we've actually used on some of the tracks and other times there would be unisons or there'll be one guitar playing melody. Basically we have ample ammunition to do what we want. We've got a lot of ammo there!"

Fans breathed a huge sigh of relief, and tried their best to overlook the six-year hiatus in the band's fortunes. By the end of the decade the metal world was once more appreciative of classic bands that had fallen by the wayside a few years earlier, and there was a lucrative place available for mega-tours from bands such as Maiden.

Of the changes in line-up, Gers mused: "First, Bruce wanted to leave. If someone had told me that we wanted to kick Bruce out, I wouldn't have stayed, but it was his decision to move on to other things. In that period we sat and thought if we wanted to go on without him, since in a band the singer is the frontman, which means in front of the band, something like the face of the band. When he leaves, you lose a great deal of your identity, and you must have great strength to redefine your identity. Iron Maiden have their identity, but Bruce was their face and it was hard to substitute him.

"Blaze came. There's no comparison between Bruce's and

Blaze's voice. Even he [Blaze] admits this. What's important is that he loved the band and gave his best to it. Bruce has an incredible range of almost three octaves. There was no chance, therefore, that Blaze could have reached Bruce's standards, and that had a bigger cost for the live shows. On the other hand, Bruce's technique is definitely greater, because, try as he might, Blaze didn't have the technical foundations Bruce has."

Janick added: "I believe every album of ours brings new elements. With time, everyone changes as a person, resulting in us bringing different ideas in the band. If you listen to every Iron Maiden album, you will see great differences. Can you compare Killers with Somewhere In Time or Seventh Son with The X Factor? They have different aesthetics. You can consider one better than the other, but they have different elements. This happens with every record, because we do not define a style of writing, but we compose as we feel... most Iron Maiden releases are different from each other, yet 100% Iron Maiden...

"Any band that survives more than two to three years follows a 'rollercoaster' career. You have highs and lows. You've just got to go through them and follow the train. You shouldn't pretend to be something you are not. If you love what you're doing and are sincere with yourself and the people that listen to your music, you survive. We went through a big period in the mid-90s when we were out of fashion. But we were playing in packed venues and 80,000 crowds at festivals. The fact that we were considered out of fashion didn't interest us. In any case, we were never really in fashion, although there were cases when we were on the radio or the TV, more out of luck rather than anything else I'd say. We play rock – popularity is the media's job."

Of the three-guitar setup, Gers explained: "Musically, I think everybody in this band can play their instruments very well. Each one of the three guitar players in this band could be the

main guitarist of the band. There is no doubt about that, and our intention is to make the band sound better with the three guitar players, and that's a challenge. Sometimes you simply don't have to play because you don't need to put too many guitars on some parts. We don't want to destroy our songs with too big guitar walls... We know how well we are playing and we know that we do our best. So you come up with some ideas you believe in and you try to make it sound great – the best sound you can get."

Of capturing the three guitars in the studio, he went on: "We wanted a live sound, so we went in without a click track or anything like that and just recorded this album live, where we are our best. Because of that, this album has a live sound which sounds like... it moves, it breathes and it sounds just great, I think. It's that kind of a thing that many bands don't do at the moment, because they are playing with the click tracks... Their songs simply don't breathe too much, and if you go back and listen to bands like Led Zeppelin and all those old bands you can feel that the thing is moving a little bit. Now people say, 'that's moving...!' but I think it's great because things like that should move and breathe a little bit."

Asked if Bruce had rejuvenated the band when he rejoined, Murray said: "Absolutely it did. We did a couple of albums when Blaze came in the band, but when we heard Bruce was interested in rejoining the band... It was like OK – let's put this together. Then we did Brave New World, which was a great reunion album... then we've gone from strength to strength with Dance Of Death. The creativity is there and we're having fun playing. So, this is definitely not a farewell tour... We spent six weeks doing that album. You get in there and do it quick, which is a great way to do an album. When you first get it home, you play the album to death... in the car, in the bath, everywhere... But now, I don't listen to it all the time, but when I do hear it I'm very satisfied. It's a strong stand-up album with a lot of depth both lyrically and musically. I think it's a big album and when you put it on... The first time it's like 'wow!' and the more you play it it grows on you. We're very proud of the album and it's one of the strongest albums we've ever done. But obviously time will tell. It's in the hands of the fans and it's their opinion that matters most... Even when you start an album and the songs are coming together, you really don't know what shape it's taking until everything's down. It just happens naturally. We don't force the issue. We don't say this is going to be another Powerslave or this is going to be another Brave New World. It just comes out."

CHAPTER 4

MARTIN BIRCH had retired after producing a string of Maiden albums, and the band recruited Kevin Shirley in his place: as Gers said, "Nowadays there is more digital equipment, the simplicity of the past doesn't exist, and Kevin knows how to use them very skillfully. You see many people working with the mix, it's like working with an atomic bomb – you have to know exactly what to do so it doesn't blow up. The thing he has managed is to make us sound like when we are playing live. The thing that Martin Birch had managed was to avoid having a sound as a producer. He didn't bring the sound of Deep Purple, Wishbone Ash or Black Sabbath into Iron Maiden. In contrast, what Mutt Lange did with Def Leppard and Bryan Adams was to have his signature on the sound.

"Kevin has succeeded in what we wanted; he makes the band sound like Iron Maiden and doesn't try to make us sound like something of his."

Janick said of the future: "You always want to redefine yourself. You want to be good at concerts, for the people that buy your albums. The first time I played at Donington in 1982 with Ian Gillan was a top moment. If my goals had ended there, I would have stopped. But ten years later I went back. You just raise the barrier constantly higher. We try to reach new countries as well as places we have been to before, but with a fresh mood. Madison Square Garden sold out instantly! We also play huge festivals. The spark still burns in us. I always worry if anyone is going to come over to see us. We musn't take anything for granted!"

Nicko added: "We all keep fit; the secret is not only to create good music, but to take care of yourself and have the will to carry on. If I had to give the secret of Iron Maiden's longevity in one sentence, I'd say it's because we still like what we do. We're a band for the stage. We compose and record music as much as we can, but that happens so that we have the opportunity to go out on the road again... I have accepted the fact that I won't be able to go on forever. I have made a promise to myself that I will not continue if I can't perform right. As long as God allows me to do so, I'll be there. I don't want to give you the right to write one day that Nicko is too old and he must be substituted because he can't pull it off any more... When I was 18, I thought you were old at 21, when I was 21 I thought you were old at 30 – and when I was 30..."

This, however, didn't mean that Maiden had it easy when it came to recorded music. If anything, the fans were listening to their old classics with renewed fervour, which meant that the band had to try twice as hard to convince with their new music – which, with the 2000 comeback album Brave New World, was no easy task. Life was good at this point, despite the poor critical reaction to the album, as Murray told Undercover: "It feels fantastic, in fact we're only kind of halfway through [the current tour] because we recorded the album in January and February and we toured over the summer. We spent about three and a half months in Europe and North America, and basically we were doing a lot of festivals and we were doing some big shows. It was basically all the older material, except for one new song, 'Wildest Dreams' from the Dance Of Death album. We're going into rehearsals next week and it's going to be a whole new production and a whole new show... it's been a big year and we've been very successful. We still have a long way to go yet. But we're still very excited and just from the response from the Iron Maiden fans throughout the world it's been tremendous so we are very pleased."

Dance Of Death included more acoustic guitars than previous albums, explained Murray: "We've kind of used acoustics a little bit in the past, but I think Adrian, Steve and Bruce came up with the idea for that song ['Journeyman'] but we actually recorded it with electric guitars as well... we thought, let's bring in some acoustics and let's have a go at it, and it actually sounds so much better being all acoustic. We're still using some keys and synths in that particular song as well, but we thought let's do something a little bit different. We have actually never done an acoustic track, so we thought let's give it a go and I think it's a real haunting melody and it's really beautiful lyrics and stuff. It's really sweet and I think with acoustics it just gives it another variation. If you listen to the Dance Of Death album, it's a pretty full-on heavy album with a lot going on, and then you come to the very last track and it's like wow, it just brings you down. It takes you out of the album in a nice way, you know? I love acoustic stuff and it's great to be able to do it with this band and on this particular album. I think it's just a timing thing, Maiden felt we were ready to put out an all-acoustic track on an album."

The album was overshadowed by the gigantic world tour which followed it, and was perhaps evidence that the best place for a mighty band such as Maiden should be on the stage. In January 2001, for example, Maiden played a show at the Rock in Rio festival in Brazil to a crowd of 250,000. Murray laughed: "There was a quarter of a million there! We went on stage at about one o'clock in the morning because their shows are very late there, and we came off at about three or three-thirty or something, and that audience had been there all day. It's tremendous that they'd stuck by us until right at the very end, and you could just feel it, there was electricity coming off these fans. I think the [cover] picture sums it up, that was a tremendous show – we had a wonderful time out there and to be able to document it and put it on DVD and stuff like that it's been fantastic. You do a lot of shows and you film them, but sometimes it far exceeds your expectations. It has been magic and it had that buzz, and I think that the Rock In Rio DVD has it, from the sound quality to everything. It's mixed in 5.1 surround sound, so if you put that on and you listen to that on an actual system it's like being in the audience. You can actually be there!"

Of the live DVD, Harris said: "We recorded a lot of the shows in Europe and we done all the video stuff in Europe as well… At the end of the day it will probably be me editing the damn thing again! I edited Maiden England '88, Maiden Donington and Rock In Rio as well. With Rock In Rio I wanted someone else to do it, because I have a particular editing style, I wanted someone else to do it, but it didn't work out that way. I carried on and did it. Afterwards I was pretty burned out. Someone had to do it, so I did it."

Bruce summed up the band's festival reputation on BBC 6 Music, saying: "Well I suppose, Donington, we've done it three times now, and this one's certainly going to be a bit different because it's going to be less of just being a gig and there's more of an event going on. I mean the one that happened last year, the old fest there was, it has to be said, it was a bit of a disaster and gave the venue a bit of a bad name, and it's a shame really because this is completely different circumstances this time around and there's a cracking thing going on, you know, and there's carnivals and funfairs and extreme sports and go-karting and there's also an absurd amount of music!"

Harris added: "We have only good memories [of festivals], as these gigs are major events. Our longest-lasting memory is that of the '88 gig before 105,000 people. Since that time, and because of a couple of deaths in the audience, the capacity at Castle Donington has been cut down to 75,000, and it's this number that came to support us last year. We're very happy about that because Britain is in full recession. Despite the rain, we really got off, both because of the music and the atmosphere. In fact, it was a bit better than in '88 'cause we didn't have any stage fright! The concert was filmed by eight 35mm cameras... We knew that it was going to be a special night. And now, we have the film!"

Bruce told writer Fredrik Hjelm: "The Rock In Rio album is gonna turn into a Maiden classic because it is one show, no overdubs, and it sounds great! It sounds really, really strong. It was the last show of the Brave New World tour, it was... broadcast live on TV to over 100 million people... it was a great place to do a live DVD and CD. So that is why we decided to do the recording in Rio, and since it was only one show, we knew we had to do it right, so there was a lot of pressure on stage, knowing we've only got one shot at this. Fortunately, we got it right!"

Of the band's many live albums, Dickinson said: "Live After Death was assembled from three nights at Long Beach, with different tracks being selected from different nights. It was also messed around with a bit. Some of the backing tracks were fine, but Adrian's guitar was way out of tune on one or two songs, so we went into a studio here in LA and did some guitar overdubs and I think I even did some vocal overdubs on 'Run To The Hills' and some other bits. All these years I felt Live After Death as being the ultimate live Maiden record, that's why it's nice to have Rock In Rio. This has a vocal performance on it of which I'm a lot more proud than Live After Death. It's shitloads better, singing-wise. Whether or not it will replace Live After Death in the affections of everybody is more difficult to say, because a record like that is more a product of its time. The same goes for Number Of The Beast... it wouldn't matter if we did an album that was twice as good as that record tomorrow, it would still never be Number Of The Beast."

Janick Gers told writer Luxi Lahtinen: "I think that a lot of people think that you first name the album and then you write the songs, but it doesn't happen like that way at all. We are doing what we've got, and then we write some songs and the ideas come up. And in the end of it you look at all the song titles, you look what you have got, what it's representing, what the album is all about and what it could be. Like on, for example, Brave New World, we think that Brave New World would be a great album title. The image of the songs we did back then. We could see Eddie doing this and that. There is the same feeling here with this new album. The initiation of Brave New World could be really good because it's... quite progressive, and that's why it's such a fitting name for the title of this new album."

He added: "When we got together, we had a feeling of the album, and then we kind of put the ideas down – that title could

be a good description of what this album is all about and where we are now. And in the end of the day, you can feel in your mind that we've chosen a really good album title for this album. Like six months ago, we didn't know where to go with that album, but here we are now. I think if you look at the older Iron Maiden albums from Killers to Virtual XI, you realise that all those albums are all very different. When you listen to those albums you know it's Iron Maiden, but they all have different kinds of themes. It's like a big tree with lots of different fruit on it. But those are all growing on the same tree. And that's, for me, what keeps the band exciting and fun, because you never know what's going to happen next. You can never be sure about certain things, if you know what I'm saying."

Of the band's new found success, Dickinson was entirely honest, saying: "To say we're the same as we were seven years ago would be a load of rubbish. We've all got our credit cards, and can do what we want now, but in a lot of ways that's better. When you're forced by necessity to sit in a minibus for eight hours going to gigs, you tell yourself that it's really important to be like that, because that's the only way you can justify it: 'It must be really important to be like this!' Success and money gives you back some of your freedom, because for that first five years you're never outside the rock'n'roll bubble. You're either touring or shacked up in some hotel, hiring the ballroom to rehearse frantically for your next album. And the only reason you get sent to record in the Bahamas or whatever, is that you can have a bit of a holiday, rest while you work, because they're gonna send you out on the road again for nine months when it's finished... I'm not pretending you don't get pissed off with it. After our 13-month Powerslave tour, I really didn't give a shit any more. I thought if this is what it's gonna do to my head, sod it! I'll go and be a folk singer. You get sick of the routine, of trotting it out every night."

Asked about the musicians' stamina in the face of exhausting, never-ending tours, Adrian explained: "I believe it has to do with the band. We play for the audience, and we have never shortened our set to make things easier. We didn't downtune to be easier to sing. I'd say it's like a cabaret, where you go to have fun. I believe that when the time that we can't make it any more comes, we will stop. We also arrange the tour in such a way that we have days off for resting. We can't go on doing what we did in the middle of the 80s."

Bruce added: "What really does you in is America, 'cos you're bashing your head against a brick wall most nights of the week… You say the same thing every night and they go wild. They're like sheep. You really have to try hard not to become like them, or before long you'll end up writing songs about rock'n'roll… That would be terrible, 'cos there's nothing of substance to write about, it's all crap, hot air and bullshit. It's usually a bunch of irresponsible boozed-up people who're far too old to be doing that respectably, going around screwing the female population and taking their money. Rock'n'roll is a licence to be irresponsible and get paid for it… everyone has a right to be that way occasionally – you have your greatest fun when you're 'carefree' – but if you did it all the time you'd end up like a walking cliché that can't drive a car or do the laundry, that thinks eggs get boiled by room service, and can't go to a bank because they think cash comes from tour managers. I know people who honestly don't know where to buy stamps, they've been on the road so long. Writing about the rock'n'roll lifestyle? Nah! It's stupid, and Joe Walsh has done it all anyway. In many ways Spinal Tap has got it exactly right. The only sad thing is that people are laughing at HM bands, without realising that it's the whole business that's like that. Whether it's pop bands who go to the Montreaux Festival, mime for 30 minutes and then collapse of nervous exhaustion, it's all bullshit."

On being a 'corporate' rock band with management to match, Dickinson explained: "Well, if you're talking about our management, it's probably true, but if you're talking about the band, it's a load of rubbish. A corporate rock band has its soul in its chequebook and wallet, and sits there churning out music to a prearranged formula to sell the maximum number of 'units' in America... I think our management is second to none – only the Genesis management is remotely as together – but we only notice they're there when something goes wrong. You phone up and say help, the truck has broken down or one of the crew is in jail, and all of a sudden the right lawyer is there, with the right amount of money at the right time, and the guy gets out of jail. That's a good manager. People say it's cynical, but they're usually jealous that you've got your act so together... you've got to remember that we've done nine to 12 months touring with all six albums. When you work that hard, and you get virtually no support from the media, you learn to capitalise on what you've got, to give everything you do maximum impact. That's why we had those attention-grabbing album covers, so

that people would go 'Yeuch! It must be Iron Maiden.' It's only recently that the media has become interested in us, that we can make people aware of our albums without putting someone with an axe through their head on the sleeve."

Fans respected the band's integrity, as Dickinson told the NME: "They have a great time with the music, and what's important about someone is not what clothes they wear or what their haircut's like; what's important is what's inside their head. All this thing about the denim being a uniform and all that, I don't think the fans see it that way. They don't see it as a uniform but as a way to identify with other people that like heavy rock. It's like saying, I like heavy metal and I'm friendly... It's not as if people go away from our shows punching other people's heads in or chopping people up with axes because of our songs. We loathe and despise violence... we place a great deal of thought into what we play and I think a lot of people place a great deal of thought into listening to what we play."

Harris once said of Maiden's army of fans: "We had some people follow us around for the whole of our last British tour and it's not something I would've done when I was like 15, 16, no matter how much I was into a band... it frightens me in a way... there are some guys who have had Iron Maiden tattoos put onto their arms and that frightens me because it's so permanent. I said to 'em, I said, fuck, they're forever, what you going to do when you're 50 or 60, you probably won't be into us any more? They said, yeah but we're so fucking into it, the energy and we're enjoying it so much, we'll be able to remember the good times we had. That's the way they felt. It's total dedication which to me is a bit frightening. You know what I mean?"

In the late 1990s the nu-metal wave rose and Maiden had some things to say about it. Harris: "First, I'd like to know what is 'new heavy metal'... there are so many different musical elements nowadays that it's not really like traditional metal any more. In the old days, there used to be music that was very distinct from one another, and Jethro Tull was pretty remote from Black Sabbath, for instance. Having said this, there was no shame in liking both. Today, everything's changed and people have become more confined to a style, they tend not to appreciate such a wide variety of bands. They like only one style and they don't listen to anything else. I think that the music industry is to blame for this… Our singles are hits, but only for a short period of time. Our fans buy them, then they climb in the charts for a week or so, then they're replaced by something else. It's true that we're always a bit worried before the release of an album 'cause we don't know how well it'll do."

The underwhelming Dance Of Death was released in 2003, but by now Maiden's fans were getting used to the idea of their band being past their commercial peak and concentrated on supporting them live. In any case, the DVD age had arrived and Maiden and their handlers embraced it fully, backed by EMI and funded by the success of Sanctuary, which had now become a serious commercial player (although this would not last: by 2006 the company was in serious difficulty). A CD single of 'The Number Of The Beast' was reissued in aid of former drummer Clive Burr, who had been stricken in recent years by multiple sclerosis, and the excellent The Early Years documentary DVD was released.

As Steve told Rock Brigade magazine of Dance Of Death, "We went on and made the album as we always do. I think the album is a little darker and a little more theatrical, maybe. The stage show will reflect that. As to why, I'm not sure. We don't do anything upfront, really. We allow ourselves a six-week writing period and that's all we do. We don't write on the road, so we just go in with new, fresh ideas. It's difficult because it's not like we said, let's make a darker album or let's do something different. We did it in a different studio and a different city and maybe that influenced us somewhat... We recorded it from January 2003 until April 2003. Then we started touring in May and went out all summer and the album was released later on. It was a bit strange for us to go out and tour without having an album out. But we did lots of summer festivals. The whole experience was different for us because we normally do an album and then a few weeks later we go on tour behind the album."

Maiden toned down their incessant touring in the new millennium, with Harris explaining: "I think we've just come to a stage where we've been touring for 25 years with each tour lasting at least nine or 10 months. We just decided that we wanted tours now to be quality over quantity. Being realistic, we're not getting any younger and you just need to pace yourself, I suppose. Plus if we tour for say four or five months instead of nine or 10 we can carry on longer. We can play in the summer. Winter tours are more difficult. Everyone gets sick in the winter. Bruce got sick and we had to cancel and then reschedule four shows... I think it's important that you play the new material. And every album we do a new tour and we always play at least six new songs... If you look back at the history of what we've done that it's always been the case. It's a challenging set for us and it's a challenging set for them."

As Murray said, each tour is different, and the Dance Of Death jaunt especially so: "Every time we've toured it's been on the focus or strength of the new album. We could be like a cabaret band and just go out and do our old songs all the time, but the strength of Maiden has been about always moving forward. The only way to do that is to go out with the new material and we're not afraid to do that. The reaction has been great. The fans know both the old songs and the new songs... You spend a few weeks rehearsing, but you have to take it out onstage in front of a live audience and that changes the pace of everything. But we're well settled into it with the songs. This is... one of

the most theatrical things we've ever put together visually. So, the songs translate to the stage very well. Dance Of Death itself starts off very moody and melancholy, but it gets very heavy. There's a lot of light and shade. We don't go out on stage for nearly two hours and bang bang bang. There's a lot of subtle quiet things happening. Yet, there's a lot of very up-tempo fast things... Maiden have always shone best in an arena. Obviously, we've played in clubs and stuff, but you just get a backline... The whole Maiden experience is the backdrop and the whole production. It also gives you space to move around. The thing with Maiden is that when we play the bigger places it kind of shines through, but we could go out with just a backline... no thrills, frills, nothing... But I think the fans expect a bit more. It's an interaction between the band and the audience. Bruce goes a long way to talking to them and getting them involved... There's a wonderful feedback. The Iron Maiden experience is an event!"

As always, Maiden were asked if the Dance... tour would be their last – but Murray said: "Once we finish this tour, we're going to take some time off. We won't be doing much till 2005. We've been everywhere twice on this tour. We need a break... we need to rest. We'll definitely be coming back out again in 2005. There's going to be another album as well. We've been documenting and videotaping this tour. So, something may be coming out from this tour... There was this thing on the internet that suggested that we were going to continue touring, but not for eight or nine-month stretches or go everywhere. Obviously, we're not getting any younger, but we can still get around everywhere... We have no intentions of a farewell tour... we will be continuing."

CHAPTER 5

IN 2005 Maiden played on the massive summer Ozzfest tour run by Black Sabbath singer Ozzy Osbourne's wife Sharon. However, the final date was marred by controversy when the band were pelted with eggs and forced to endure power cuts during the set: a row erupted between Sharon and Smallwood when it was revealed that the former had orchestrated the egg-throwing after alleged comments made by Dickinson towards Ozzy across the course of the Ozzfest. The issue remains unclear to this day, but Smallwood fumed at the time that it was the most unprofessional thing he had ever seen. Maiden – who retained their dignity throughout, largely by refraining from joining in the comments made by either party – finished off 2005 with a live album and DVD, Death On The Road.

A completely unexpected return to recorded form came in summer 2006, when Maiden released their fourteenth studio album, A Matter Of Life And Death. Much praised by critics and fans, the album undoubtedly precedes a renewed bout of touring and recording as we went to press. Harris remained sanguine as ever of the success of the new album, saying: "All I can say is that we are very lucky, we're still very strong in most countries all over the world. If our popularity in one country goes down a bit, it goes up in another country, so we're not relying on one country in particular to keep up our popularity. Whereas some bands rely heavily on success in Japan, we're not in that position, fortunately. [The X Factor] sold well over a million copies worldwide, but a lot of people here in the States thought we just vanished. That's why touring for us is very important... and we don't really make money touring, we pretty much break even."

Retirement looms nowadays, but then it always has in this most ephemeral of careers. Of the future, Harris said as far back as 1982: "I just want to play on stage and enjoy myself for as long as I can. Let's face it, we all get old, and I know that I won't be able to deliver this kind of performance forever... in 10 years' time I won't be able to do this, and I tell you I don't even want to think about that day. It's gonna be a sad day when that happens. It's like, all it is, I really get off on what I'm doing and I'm sure a lot of the younger fans would love to be in my position and maybe in a few years they will be."

As McBrain laughed when the subject of retirement came up: "I'm 51 years old now but I can still rock! Just as everyone else in the band. And I'm the most handsome guy in the band! Only joking. Seriously, we love our fans, and we love what we do. We're like a big, expanded family. I mean, there's many kinds of music for the kids to choose from today. Still they're loyal to us. We in Maiden have always done the same thing really, we have [never] changed our principles. And still so many enjoy our music."

Asked why he had never contributed to the songwriting, Nicko mused: "I don't know, probably I'm just lazy! Maybe the self-esteem isn't very good either; there are such a lot of good songwriters in the band. Recently I've written a few songs with my wife, and I got interested in playing bass. 'New Frontier' wasn't first supposed to be a Maiden song, but my wife told me to show it to the band. So I did, and it made it on the album, after having been re-worked by me and Adrian. Bruce also wrote some new lyrics for it... I listen mainly to old stuff, like Eric Clapton, Deep Purple, Pink Floyd and Led Zeppelin. But my son likes new bands! He often asks me to play Brave New World in the car. Besides, I've never seen Maiden fully as a metal band. More of a progressive rock band. A little underground. At least we were in the 80s. Back then many people were scared

of us, of our lyrics and the covers with Eddie. And many still question us."

The media have still never really accepted Maiden, as Murray explained: "I think with this band, they've always kind of shunned us and there's nothing we can do about it really. We just have to get on with life and carry on with playing music really, which means we've done it on our own backs. We haven't had any help from those guys and so it basically proves that you can do it, you can go out there and be successful on whatever level it is, but you don't have to have that type of exposure... Steve first formed the band in 1975, so if you go back that far it's 30 years, but with this particular line-up, it's still a long time!"

Nowadays, like Bruce, Nicko is a pilot in his spare time. Of this quintessentially rich man's hobby, he explained: "The passion of flight... I decided that I wanted to fly like an eagle! I once flew with a guy in the Channel Islands out of Jersey and it was in February 1986. We hit some supercool air and the airframe decided to ice up. It was a fairly heavy 30 minutes of flight limping back to the airport. The engine also decided that it would rough run, that means that ice gets into the carbs and starves the fuel to the engine. We made it back and when we landed we left a whole bunch of ice on the runway. It was very invigorating..."

The Discovery Channel once interviewed Bruce about his flying, which had developed so far by the end of the 1990s that he was soon ferrying band and fans to gigs: "I can only get up to 42,000 feet on a 757, so to get to the same level as Iron Maiden I'd have to get to 300,000 feet, which is the same as our crowd at Rock In Rio. That would be pretty exciting, I reckon... but unlikely at the moment... [as a child] I had a fleet of Heinkel 111s, Focke-Wulf 190s, Hurricanes, Thunderbolts, Lancasters and a Sunderland, not to mention a plastic zeppelin. Every now and then one would plunge to a fiery doom from my bedroom window after being modified by cotton wool and lighter fluid... It took me ages to pluck up the courage to have a go at flying, mainly because I thought I couldn't cope with the academic side of the exams (I was hopeless at maths and physics at school). After my first flight I just decided that I would do whatever it took to get up to speed and pass the ground school. I spent a year doing the academic exams and the flying exams. I already had a private licence and had a reasonable amount of experience. Once you have a commercial licence and the instrument rating to go with it, then you are in a position to try and badger people into letting you fly their airplanes. The next hurdle is getting a job and passing the ground and flight exams to fly jet aircraft – I found that very tough."

Of the piloted trips in the wake of September 11, 2001, he explained: "Almost every pilot I know regrets the fact that we are not allowed to have people visit the flight deck anymore. If we could let people up front, then we would. Where are the pilots of tomorrow going to have their first experience of flight? So many young kids became pilots after visiting the flight deck. In some ways TV shows... are the only ways of telling people what a great job it is... I've got to hand it to the 727 crew. They happily let me take off, whizz around the Everglades and do a touch and go plus three full stop landings in it. I really loved the 727, but I was also very surprised at the Airbus A320. Both are pioneering aircraft from different eras, but I found both of them very harmonious in their design... After the aerodynamics of swept wings began to be understood, it was powerplants that were the big frontier. The 747 was plagued by its lack of power early on, and it's only now that engines have been developed that are powerful enough to make super jumbos a reality."

Of a possible collaboration with Dan Spitz of Anthrax and Dave Ellefson of Megadeth, Nicko explained: "It all started from Dan who has been my friend for years. Our wives meet up at church often and we hang out as well. He played some ideas that he had recorded in his basement to me and suggested to me to compose some ideas of my own so we can mix them. It took us a long time, but his very good ideas turned into good songs. So one day he calls me and explains to me that he had come in contact with Vanilla Ice, because he was religious as well, and speaking about his songs, he told him to join in. I was very wary before I had heard the songs, but believe me, the guy knows what rap means. In some parts, his voice is amazing. It's not that easy for me to describe it to you, as it's not Iron Maiden, it's not Anthrax and it's not rap. It's a combination of ideas with a dynamic result. I have never heard of anything like it in the past… Dan was so excited about the idea, that he was telling it to everybody. On the other hand, Dave didn't want anything to leak, because he wasn't sure if he wanted to join or not. He helped us a lot and I think he would have stayed until the idea was complete, but the way things developed and it got known didn't sit well with him and he left. We'll see what happens…

Maybe sometime we will complete it, after the tour with Iron Maiden, we will see."

Asked if he had ever thought Maiden would evolve into a long-term project, Nicko said: "To be honest with you, no. I didn't think how long it would last, if it would be five or 10 years. I just hoped it would last as long as possible. And when I was with the band for a while, then the success started to build, and the fanbase was growing, I knew it was something unique. Of course there are bands who are longer in the business, like Deep Purple and the Rolling Stones, but we have something extra, namely Eddie! And he has to be the face which fits the music and the band. Actually we're touring just to show him to the people, hahaha. Because if he's not present at our concert, the fans get mad... In the early days when we finished a song, we would go to the pub, and celebrate. Now we only do that when we are finished with all the songs. Otherwise we wouldn't have the time to record an album. We present our ideas, and we work them out. Usually Steve and I work out our parts first, and then the rest of the band comes in."

McBrain added: "With us, you never know what you're gonna get. Through the years we wrote so many songs, and we will never be able to play them all. We have 13 studio albums, so there's so much material. Personally I would love to play 'Alexander The Great' live. That's one of the few epic songs we never played live. Now that we have three guitar players, there's no reason why we shouldn't play it live. So my vote goes to that song. But obviously we go on tour to promote the new album. So we will play many songs from that. It features a lot of long songs, so we are unsure how we're gonna fit that in, because you cannot play too many of these long songs. Normally we will play two-thirds of the new album. Of course we will play a few of our regular songs, like 'Iron Maiden', 'The Number Of The Beast', maybe 'Run to the Hills'. Because people want to hear those songs. Just like 'Hallowed Be Thy Name'. It's unthinkable we don't play that song. It's my favourite Iron Maiden song."

After such a lengthy career, Harris was asked if he ever felt nostalgic for the old days. He laughed this suggestion off, remarking: "No, not really. I don't do nostalgia. I never feel depressed or anything. I remember when the songs were played, but it doesn't affect me any more than that. On the other hand, I'm quite sad that some songs could never be recorded. During Maiden's early days, we had very few photos of the band 'cause we couldn't afford them. Except from memories, we virtually have nothing left from that time. Now, I have to say that I have many many photos and films, but only from the Number Of The Beast tour onwards. The beginnings of Iron Maiden are lost forever... At times, what was very clear at the time doesn't seem to be any more. Times change, you evolve, you change your mind, and you forget things. But, when I think about it, I think that Maiden never screwed up. Our work is varied, and that's a good thing. Some little details can be annoying, but, as a whole, everything's quite satisfactory. Every time you release a live album or a video, you feel like you've turned a page and that you're about to start on new projects. They may not be major ones, but you do get this feeling of novelty when you start on another chapter."

Of his role in the band – which some might say is an autocratic one – Harris once explained: "Maybe that's what people think because I started Maiden, but I don't think I'm a leader. All the band-members have their say and all of them are heard. There's no star in this band 'cause Iron Maiden is a whole. I must admit that I've thought of [doing a solo album] a few times... but never really seriously. The problem is I don't sing! I'd need to find a singer and I would quite like that... If I was to record a solo album, it would be either "sub-Maiden", or progressive rock."

He went on: "I'd rather have us considered a great rock band, and I think that the others also feel the same way. To be a rock band isn't just about the usual heavy metal clichés. We don't like stereotypes and we always try to renew ourselves. This is why we're good, and I think that a few other bands should take a leaf out of our book... most heavy metal bands won't admit it because they have some sort of tunnel vision. They were influenced by three or four of our songs and they claim they know nothing of the rest of our compositions. However, Iron Maiden remains unique. On the other hand, I'm happy to know that Maiden have been an influence. I take it as a compliment... We are a real good team and we get on really well with each other. It's about five mates pursuing the same goal. Before, it obviously was quite different, but now we all evolve together and the musical changes that occur affect all of us. It's a different experience, and quite an enjoyable one."

Of his age, Harris observed: "I like to stay with my family, go on holiday, play football and write. Nowadays, we can afford to have some free time and that's really nice. As our tours are organised differently, we have more time for non-musical activities. We recharge our batteries in order to give even more on stage. Not so long ago, we had to have a year off 'cause we were burned out. We had the feeling we'd been working for a decade before we could take a break. Now, after some rest, we can get back into it more refreshed! I can write without any pressure and so I can more easily express my ideas and feelings... It's a real luxury and I'd rather work like this than have a full rock'n'roll life... I have become more aware of what's happening on the planet, and mostly since I'm a father. Since I've had kids, I think that I've become a better person, much more sensitive than I used to be. This is all due to my kids. It really sickens me when I hear that there are lunatics who chop kids into bits with an axe. Before, such news would have upset me, but now that I have kids of my own, it really makes me sick... We have a few regrets, but as a whole, we're pretty happy. We are very grateful for what's happened to us, and what keeps happening. It's great 'cause each album was a step in a progression. On top of that, we became increasingly popular. We never were interested in anything else but music, and I am not ashamed of any of our albums."

Dave Artwood, 2007

TRACK BY TRACK ANALYSIS

THIS SONG-BY-SONG run-through of Iron Maiden's recorded catalogue seeks to provide a clear, unbiased assessment of each of their albums. Each song and album is given a rating out of five as follows:

Absolutely essential: ★ ★ ★ ★ ★
Excellent: ★ ★ ★ ★
Average: ★ ★ ★
Poor: ★ ★
Terrible: ★

Compilations and live albums only get a summary rather than a track-by-track analysis.

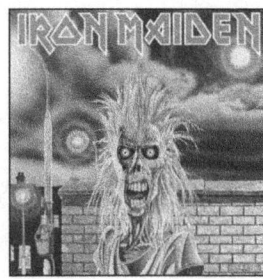

IRON MAIDEN
(Album, 1980)

The group's debut album named after the band themselves. The album is considered as a classic heavy metal album and contains one of the group's most recognisable tracks: Iron Maiden.

Prowler ★ ★ ★

Prowler was the first track from the band's debut album. It was never released as a single but is believed to be one of the first songs written by Steve Harris. The song was played at almost every one of the band's live tours. The immortal gambit may sound a little worn after so many years, but it still epitomises the raw and aggressive sound of the then-really 'new' New Wave Of British Heavy Metal as much or better than many other classic songs of its era.

Remember Tomorrow ★ ★

Harris described Remember Tomorrow as "An old stage favourite which the crowds were always into". Paul Di'Anno said that the song was actually written in tribute of his grandfather. "Tears for remembrance and tears for joy", sings Di'Anno on this underrated album track, on which the band do their best to sound profound.

Running Free ★ ★ ★ ★

Running Free was the band's first single release. It was released in February of 1980 and was well received by the critics, however the song never charted. From its classic Harris bass intro to the ridiculously over-the-top youth-gone-wild lyrics and Paul Di'Anno's untamed bark, 'Running Free' is one song which all youthful metal fans (no matter what age nowadays) will recall as a genre- and epoch-defining moment. Genius, in a simple way, even if it didn't betray the slightest hint of the epic musical progression to come.

Transylvania ★ ★

Transylvania was a track composed by Steve Harris in tribute to his local club The Cart and Horses. On a walk home from the club he decided to think about songs and pitched it to the band the next day. An instrumental on which – even in these early days – the band sound pretty dexterous, 'Transylvania' is far from the vampire epic you'd think it was from the title. A shame, really…

Phantom Of The Opera ★ ★ ★ ★

Phantom of the Opera was based not on the famous musical but on the original French novel by Gaston Leroux. The song is actually best known in the UK for its use in a Lucozade commercial in the 1980s. Among the first ever ambitious, extended epics which Steve and his band of merry men ever wrote, 'Phantom…' remains remarkably fresh-sounding despite its vintage. It's also one of the few songs which make it apparent that Di'Anno could really sing when he wanted to: listen out for his vibrato, for example – wielded well rather than laboriously. There's a gorgeous bass solo moment, composed of tricky triads, and some simple power-chord arpeggios that are all the more devastating for their simplicity. This song has something for everyone, not least its thundering central riff (the Maiden 'gallop' in essence), which made it perfect for soundtracking a Lucozade commercial.

Strange World ★ ★ ★
Strange World was intended as a follow on piece from the instrumental Transylvania. The song was never released as a single but is a popular album track amongst fans. If Steve Harris' lyrics came primarily from nightmares (as Bruce has mentioned a few times), then 'Strange World' must have come from a very pleasant dream indeed. It's completely idyllic…

Charlotte The Harlot ★ ★ ★
This song is the first appearance of Charlotte the Harlot who appears in four Iron Maiden tracks across the albums. She is apparently based on a prostitute called High Hill Lil from the Walthamstow area of London. "Taking so many men to your room, don't you feel no remorse?" inquires Di'Anno in a lyric that is less Harrisian poetry than pub banter. Still, Charlotte has gone down in history as a metal icon, right up there with Eddie.

Iron Maiden ★ ★ ★
Iron Maiden was one of the first videos to ever be played on MTV. Along with Run to the Hills it is one of the band's most recognisable songs. The song has featured in every one of Iron Maiden's live performances. A classic title song (like Motörhead's 'Motörhead', come to think of it), 'Iron Maiden' is simple but effective – the urban tale of the woman who 'can't be fought, can't be sought'.

Conclusion

Iron Maiden isn't a perfect album, but then how many debut albums – from metal bands or otherwise – are? What the record does do with great ease is demonstrate the vast potential of this as yet untried band, with their nascent virtuosity still yet to evolve fully.

Overall rating: ★ ★ ★

RUNNING FREE
(Single, 1980)

Tracklisting: Running Free / Burning Ambition

A defining heavy metal single of the era, 'Running Free' was many fans' initiation into Iron Maiden, and by extension to metal itself. Venom ushered in a new era with 'In League With Satan' in 1981 and Metallica with the compilation track 'Hit The Lights' two years later – both genre-defining releases, but neither quite as important in terms of their cultural impact as 'Running Free'.

Overall rating: ★ ★ ★ ★

SANCTUARY
(Single, 1980)

Tracklisting: Sanctuary / Drifter / I've Got The Fire

Another undisputed classic from Maiden's earliest recording incarnation, 'Sanctuary' remains a sing-along set favourite as well as lending its name to manager Rod Smallwood's record label and management stable. One of those songs that any metalhead has to know…

Overall rating: ★ ★ ★ ★

WOMEN IN UNIFORM
(Single, 1980)

Tracklisting: Women In Uniform / Invasion / Phantom Of The Opera

Sexist? Clumsy? Teenage in nature? Of course! An ode to the suited ladies in authority that populate many a sweaty teenager's night-time fantasies, 'Women In Uniform' was typical of the slightly pathetic sexual nature of some of the early NWOBHM tunes (in a pitiful attempt to ape their AOR and stadium-rock counterparts). Nowadays it sounds stupid but nostalgically attractive, not least for Paul Di'Anno's whining growl. The fact that the epic (and frankly superior) 'Phantom Of The Opera' appears on the B-side is an added bonus.

Overall rating: ★ ★ ★

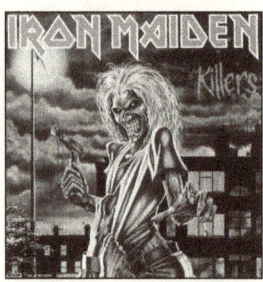

KILLERS
(Album, 1981)

The group's second album, it was released in February of 1981. Wrathchild is one of the most popular songs on the album and was recently featured in the Playstation game Guitar Hero. The album also features two entirely instrumental tracks.

The Ides Of March ★ ★ ★
An instrumental album track and like previous albums another skilfully-executed instrumental from the band, 'The Ides Of March' doesn't bear any resemblance to its title but does sound suitably ominous in parts.

Wrathchild ★ ★ ★
Wrathchild is considered as one of the bands classic songs

and has been covered by many bands and featured in adverts and video games. The song still features in live performances and is usually the first song of the band's live set. A classic Maiden song from this early stage and one which gave its name to an unfortunate set of hair-metal gimps on both sides of the Atlantic… but that's not Iron Maiden's fault.

Murders In The Rue Morgue ★ ★ ★
"Someone call the gendarmes!" (the first and only use of that word in any heavy metal song to date). This particular piece of trickery is among the first to be inspired by the world of classical literature.

Another Life ★ ★
Another song in which Di'Anno sings of lying on his bed, 'Another Life' is a short, interesting album filler.

Genghis Khan ★ ★
The mighty Asiatic serial killer would no doubt have been highly complimented to learn that 754 years after his death, a British heavy metal band would write a song about him. The song, however wasn't ever released as a single and isn't regarded as a classic.

Innocent Exile ★ ★
There's no mystery here – 'Innocent Exile' is a song about a man who's innocent and he's in exile. You see? It's not complicated stuff, this. Not yet, anyway.

Killers ★ ★
The albums title track, Killers was never the success that the group intended it to be. The song was written by Steve Harris. The song is a reasonably detailed tale of taking somebody's life and then worrying about it quite a lot, 'Killers' is a morality tale of sorts, complete with shouts of 'Oh yeah!' and attempts at demonic laughter.

Prodigal Son ★ ★
"I've got this curse, I'm turning to bad!" whines Di'Anno in this slightly obscure tale of a geezer sinking into depression. The music, though, is all Maiden – dexterous and ambitious.

Purgatory ★ ★
Purgatory was the only song originally released from the Killers album but it was entirely unsuccessful failing to break into the Top 50 of the UK singles chart. With its themes of levitation, spiritual elevation and general ambient weirditude, it seems that Steve had eaten too much Stilton before going to bed one night and writing 'Purgatory' in the morning.

Twilight Zone ★ ★ ★
The spirit world, yielding up a ghost three years after its human death? Check. A song about said ghost's thoughts on the nature of existence? Check.

Drifter ★ ★ ★
A positive song for a change, with the central narrator promising to hold his lover (or child) securely, 'Drifter' is a great way to round off the album.

Conclusion
Killers stepped up a notch from the youthful extravagance of Iron Maiden, but it wasn't until the advanced excellence of The Number Of The Beast that Steve Harris and Iron Maiden really found their identity as songwriters or musicians. With that in mind, Killers should really be seen as part two of the two-part Paul Di'Anno saga: a reflection of his adequate, rather than excellent, skills, and a souvenir of a fun but unsophisticated era that had no real place on the British music scene after about 1982.

Overall rating: ★ ★ ★

TWILIGHT ZONE
(Single, 1981)

Tracklisting: Twilight Zone / Wrathchild

Perhaps a slightly unusual selection of single from the 'Killers' album, but nonetheless, 'Twilight Zone' conveys the message to the fanbase that Iron Maiden can write high-quality material.

Overall rating: ★ ★ ★

PURGATORY
(Single, 1981)

Tracklisting: Purgatory / Genghis Khan

More spirit-world musings from the Maiden, as the next single from Killers sees Paul Di'Anno depart for a life in a series of second-rate bar bands and appearances as a talking head in Iron Maiden documentaries.

Overall rating: ★ ★ ★

MAIDEN JAPAN
(EP, 1981)

Tracklisting: Running Free / Remember Tomorrow / Killers / Innocent Exile

A useful early reminder of the powerful live Iron Maiden show, Maiden Japan – which seemed to have been recorded in a different universe, such was the unknown quantity of far-off territories such as the Far East back in those days – is a simple four-song souvenir of the Di'Anno line-up and its moderate charms. The singer is on typically laddish form throughout, while the rest of the band outdo him relatively easily. The writing was on the wall… and it was in Japanese.

Overall rating: ★ ★ ★

THE NUMBER OF THE BEAST
(Album, 1982)

Number of the Beast is regarded as the album which made the band into a household name. The album thrust the group into a worldwide stage and established them at the top of the heavy metal genre. Of all the songs on the album, "The Number of the Beast", "Run to the Hills" and "Hallowed Be Thy Name" remain on the set lists of nearly all the band's tours, with the latter two often used to close a show. All three songs have been released as singles in various forms. The album is also Iron Maiden's highest selling album worldwide with over 14 million sales estimated.

Invaders ★ ★ ★
With its mentions of 'Nordic fighting men' and longboats, it's clear that The Number Of The Beast's opening track is not going to be about market gardening – it's about war!

Children Of The Damned ★ ★ ★
A Revelations-style elegy about a kid whose face peels off – had Steve been watching The Omen? – 'Children Of The Damned' is still a classic after all these (wasted) years.

The Prisoner ★ ★ ★ ★
A classic, even without McGoohan's introduction. 'The Prisoner' remains one of those songs that you have to know inside out if you want to call yourself an Iron Maiden fan.

22 Acacia Avenue ★ ★ ★
It's Charlotte the Harlot again, not having a good time as Bruce sings about her multiple abuses at the hands of evil clients. Still, it works out fine – she is rescued at the song's end.

The Number Of The Beast ★ ★ ★ ★
The second single released from the album and arguably the band's most popular and commercial song. The song reached number 18 in the UK charts, a great performance for a heavy metal song. The band had asked the famous horror film actor Vincent Price to read the intro text. However, according to Dickinson, Price refused to do it for anything less than £25,000. They had heard of someone who read ghost stories at Capital Radio and got him to do it. The man was a theatre actor named Barry Clayton who had no interest in Maiden, but they asked him to put on a Vincent Price kind of voice. The song caused controversy in the USA with Southerners accusing the band of being Satanists from the use of the 666 lyric in the chorus. The best song Iron Maiden had written in a while thanks to that insistent guitar drone and vocal melody that wouldn't quit, the album's title track is sophisticated from such a young band.

Run To The Hills ★ ★ ★ ★
Run to the Hills was the band's first single release from the album. The lyrics poignantly discuss the impact of colonials on Native Amercian Indians in the 19th Century. It was ranked as the 27th best song of all time by VH1. The song features on video games including Guitar Hero, SSZ and Grand Theft Auto. It is a great, great song, more akin to a pop tune than a metal anthem (although it's both, of course), 'Run To The Hills' is responsible for the ascent of Iron Maiden. Without it, their climb to prominence would have been much slower.

Gangland ★ ★
Contract killings, jailbirds, Adrian Smith co-writing credits –

yes, 'Gangland' was pretty juvenile. Not that this would have mattered if it had been as gripping as 'Run To The Hills'…

Total Eclipse ★ ★ ★

A song about, uh, a total eclipse, 'Total Eclipse' pulls in some spooky biblical references to scare the kids and, all in all, does the job.

Hallowed Be Thy Name ★ ★ ★

The song describes a man's journey to the gallows and a fear of dying. The song has been released as both a live and studio recording. It made the top 100 Metal Songs of all time in a VH1 survey. The use of rhyming 'error' with 'terror', 'Hallowed Be Thy Name' is the story of a bloke being marched out to the firing squad. It's not pretty, but then it's not supposed to be.

Conclusion

Although not every song on The Number Of The Beast has 'classic' stamped on it, the album's impact on the metal scene and its enduring presence – influencing countless Satanic bands (pseudo or otherwise) with its sleeve art and demonic lyrics – makes it one of the finest metal albums ever made. The outstanding songs – the title track, 'The Prisoner', 'Run To The Hills', 'Hallowed Be Thy Name' – will endure for decades, even if tricks such as Patrick McGoohan's introduction to 'The Prisoner' and various other hokey elements have aged poorly in the interim.

Overall rating: ★ ★ ★ ★

RUN TO THE HILLS
(Single, 1982)

Tracklisting: Run To The Hills / Total Eclipse

Not only Iron Maiden's breakthrough single but the release

that signalled to the world that British metal was back – and back in large, commercially viable chunks – 'Run To The Hills' was funny (check the cowboys'n'Injuns video), catchy and the ultimate banging-your-first-in-the-air tune.

Overall rating: ★ ★ ★

THE NUMBER OF THE BEAST
(Single, 1982)

Tracklisting: The Number Of The Beast / Remember Tomorrow

Who shall argue with this superlative bit of vinyl? Perhaps only the legions of moronic American Christians who burned Maiden's Number…-era releases in the streets. Still, all the more power to the band, who had turned themselves into a bona fide musical phenomenon by now.

Overall rating: ★ ★ ★ ★

PIECE OF MIND
(Album, 1983)

Piece of Mind was a 1983 album release for the band. It was a classic follow up album to Number of the Beast and was also successful during the peak era of Heavy Metal. In 1990 Steve Harris said that he thought Piece of Mind was the group's best album and the sales figures worldwide have exceeded 13 million. The album was the first to feature Nicko McBrain on drums.

Where Eagles Dare ★ ★ ★

The song marks the first use of drummer Nicko McBrain with a marvellous drum solo. The song Where Eagles Dare is based on the war film and book of the same name from 1967. The band have all said that this song justified their decision to add Nicko to the band. Blatantly pinching its theme from the film of the same name – weren't Maiden quite the culture vultures, eh? – 'Where Eagles Dare' even locates its story of daring and intrigue in the Bavarian Alps, helpfully.

Revelations ★ ★ ★

Revelation has become a fan favourite and is frequently included in live sets. It was also written solely by Bruce Dickinson, one of very few songs to be solo written without the imput of Harris. Combining biblical exhortations with one part riffage and two parts earnest lyricism, 'Revelations' shows that Maiden had deep things on their minds back in 1982.

Flight Of Icarus ★ ★

Flight of Icarus was the first single released from the 1983 album. It was also the first Iron Maiden single to receive extensive airplay in the United States. The song reached number 11 on the UK singles chart but amazingly peaked at 8 on the US singles chart. Literally the story of the flight of Icarus – who fashioned some wings of wax but fell to his doom after flying too close to the sun, implausibly – this song is worth your investigation, but only just.

Die With Your Boots On ★ ★ ★

A collaboration song between Harris, Dickinson and then guitarist Adam Smith the song is about the impact prophecies and predictions can have on a man's life. More horror stories from Revelations or the popular cinematic equivalent thereof, 'Die With Your Boots On' – although its title makes it sound like a war anthem – is anything but.

The Trooper ★ ★ ★ ★

The second single released from the album, The Trooper is

about the Crimean War and the Battle of Balaclava. The song peaked at number 28 in the US charts. The obvious classic on this slightly mixed-up album, 'The Trooper' does what Maiden do best – i.e. sing about swashbuckling heroism and the horrors of warfare – in inimitable style, unforgettable lead riff and all.

Still Life ★ ★ ★
"I've no doubt that you think I'm off my head," sings Bruce, doing well to get all that out and still pose on stage. The song is a strange one, perhaps in keeping with the theme of mental instability that pervades this album.

Quest For Fire ★ ★
Cavemen trying to make fire? Perfect lyrical inspiration for a metal band, I'm sure you'll agree – and in fact, it works more or less admirably.

Sun And Steel ★ ★
The idea that a warrior lives life fully aware of his own death is one that inevitably crosses most headbangers' minds from time to time, not least due to this rather good song.

To Tame A Land ★ ★ ★
To Tame a Land is the closing track from the album. The track has only been performed live once on the 1983 World Piece Tour. Originally to be titled 'Dune' after the sci-fi novel of the same name, the lyrics of 'To Tame A Land' will be instantly familiar to anyone who knows what 'Kwisatz Haderach' means.

Conclusion
Piece Of Mind has sterling cover art – Eddie, chained up in a mental institution's padded cell, raving and frothing against the bonds that hold him – but doesn't match this excellence in its grooves. There's nothing particularly wrong with it, and in fact quite a few of the tunes have survived a couple of decades in the

live set – but it doesn't match up to the glories that followed or the sheer extravagance of the album which preceded it.

Overall rating: ★ ★ ★

FLIGHT OF ICARUS
(Single, 1983)

Tracklisting: Flight Of Icarus / I've Got The Fire

The tale of the crispy-winged ground-hitter made a good single, accompanied as it was by the dexterously performed anthem 'I've Got The Fire'.

Overall rating: ★ ★ ★

THE TROOPER
(Single, 1983)

Tracklisting: The Trooper / Cross Eyed Mary

More single-sized genius from the Maiden, with a song that is covered by upstart metal bands like Trivium to this day. While the B-side is best forgotten about, it does indicate that Maiden had a sense of humour, unlike their mad-eyed detractors across the pond...

Overall rating: ★ ★ ★

POWERSLAVE
(Album, 1984)

Following on from the huge successes of both Number of the Beast and Piece of Mind, Powerslave was perhaps slightly disappointing in comparison.

It was released in September of 1984 and Aces High and 2 Minutes to Midnight were the only songs released as singles. It interestingly contains a tribute to the Coleridge poem The Rime of the Ancient Mariner. The tour was called the World Slavery Tour.

Aces High ★ ★ ★

The second single released from the Powerslave album, the song tells the story of a British RAF pilot during the Battle of Britain. The song reached number 20 on the British singles chart. The song has recently featured on the video game Madden 2010, an American football game, as a menu song. Only someone with serious knowledge of WW2 air battles ("Ten ME-109s coming out of the sun!") could have written this sabre-rattling tune. It's rather good, too.

2 Minutes To Midnight ★ ★ ★ ★

The most successful song on the album, 2 Minutes to Midnight was the album's opening single and reached number 11 in the UK singles chart as well as number 25 in the American charts. The song has considerable references to the Doomsday clock, the clock used by nuclear scientists to determine how close to nuclear war the world is. The clock reached 23:58 in 1953 hence the song title. This is a weird song, '2 Minutes To Midnight' is a great song – I defy anyone not to emulate that full-throated wail on the chorus – but doesn't let you know it until that selfsame chorus, as it begins with a slightly mundane monotone. Don't worry, though – after the first minute it's like coming home. Welcome to Maidenville.

Losfer Words ★ ★

Another Maiden album, another useful instrumental to calm the nerves before the big fighting songs recommence…

Flash Of The Blade ★ ★ ★
The smell of resined leather, the steely iron mask? Either Bruce was referring to his fencing skills (he was No. 7 in the UK rankings, you know) or a grisly death at the point of a sword: either way, it was stirring stuff.

The Duellists ★ ★ ★ ★
More swordfighting with two aggrieved chaps taking it out on each other, 'The Duellists' does the trick – of depicting old-school violence in an old-school metal way – with aplomb.

Back In The Village ★ ★ ★
Mental instability rears its head once more as the central character recalls seeing things no-one should see, back in a war-stricken village from which he has escaped. Grim stuff.

Powerslave ★ ★ ★
The epic tale of an Egyptian god whose death terrifies him, 'Powerslave' ties in perfectly with Derek Riggs' cover art of a huge, malevolent sphinx and powers down the album, segueing perfectly into...

Rime Of The Ancient Mariner ★ ★ ★
A superbly self-indulgent bit of nonsense from team Harris, complete with a droning, trancelike bass figure and sound effects nicked straight from Davy Jones' locker. Who knows what the song is about, really, other than a slice of fantastical whimsy from someone (probably Bruce) who had been reading a bit of classical literature?

Conclusion
Powerslave was and remains one of Iron Maiden's finest albums, a synthesis of metallic swagger with the epic song themes and soundscapes which were rapidly becoming a key selling-point for the band. Harris was evolving well as a songwriter, most crucially, while Bruce was coming into his own as a lyricist

and frontman to match any other. An early milestone in a long career littered with such milestones.

Overall rating: ★ ★ ★ ★

2 MINUTES TO MIDNIGHT
(Single, 1984)

Tracklisting: 2 Minutes To Midnight / Rainbow's Gold / Mission From 'Arry

The obvious choice of single from the Powerslave album, '2 Minutes To Midnight' was the perfect four-minute radio song – if any radio station had been brave enough to play it in those running-scared days, that is. With only one comedy song out of the two B-sides, the buyer was doing well, too.

Overall rating: ★ ★ ★

ACES HIGH
(Single, 1984)

Tracklisting: Aces High / King Of Twilight / The Number Of The Beast (Live)

Another slab of all-out war fantasy from Steve and Bruce, this time more from the latter's Biggles-indebted point of view. You can tell from the lyrics alone – let alone the axes-aloft riffage – that the band weren't so different from their primarily male, teenage audience after all. Another perfect set of single vibes, including a remarkably decent live stab at 'The Number Of The Beast'.

Overall rating: ★ ★ ★

LIVE AFTER DEATH
(Album, 1985)

Tracklisting: Intro: Churchill's Speech / Aces High / 2 Minutes To Midnight / The Trooper / Revelations / Flight Of Icarus / Rime Of The Ancient Mariner / Powerslave / The Number Of The Beast / Hallowed By Thy Name / Iron Maiden / Run To The Hills / Running Free / Wrathchild / 22 Acacia Avenue / Children Of The Damned / Die With Your Boots On / Phantom Of The Opera

For a while, it's fair to say, Live After Death was the ultimate heavy metal live album. Adorned with a stunning sleeve depicting Eddie bursting from the grave, with hundreds of tiny details for the LP-loving fan to pore over, the record contained songs culled from three mega-shows in Long Beach. The sound of Bruce dividing the arena into halves and having each side compete in singing competitions is wholly evocative, even from two decades' distance. It's great stuff.

Overall rating: ★ ★ ★ ★

RUNNING FREE (LIVE)
(Single, 1985)

Tracklisting: Running Free (Live) / Sanctuary (Live)

A live version of the perennial 'Running Free' made perfect sense when promoting the hefty Live After Death album, especially twinned with the old-school sound of 'Sanctuary'.

Overall rating: ★ ★ ★

RUN TO THE HILLS (LIVE)
(Single, 1985)

Tracklisting: Run To The Hills (Live) / Phantom Of The Opera (Live)

A live take on 'Run To The Hills' complemented the previous issue of 'Running Free', perhaps without the balls of the studio version but still a stunning song in any format. The B-side, in fact, was the superior song this time around – a long, unhurried but still powerful song which doesn't outstay its welcome despite its length.

Overall rating: ★ ★ ★

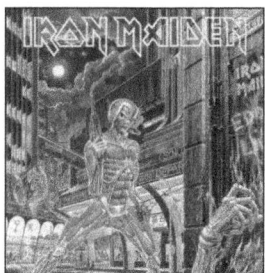

SOMEWHERE IN TIME
(Album, 1986)

This album was reasonably successful but sparked one of the big controversies which led to the departure of Bruce Dickinson in 1990. Bruce Dickinson's song material was refused in favour of the songs of guitarist Adrian Smith, who wrote the bulk of the songs identified with the album including the singles 'Wasted Years' and 'Stranger in a Strange Land'. It was also the first Iron Maiden album to feature synthesisers, both bass and guitar. Somewhere on Tour was the name of the tour which supported the album.

Caught Somewhere In Time ★ ★ ★
The theme of time passing and standing still is explored fully in this subtle song, executed with precision by a band now fully in control of their tools and rewarded with a budget to match.

Wasted Years ★ ★ ★
The first single released from the album, Waster Years was

written by guitarist Adam Smith and reached number 18 in the UK charts. Interestingly, the song refers to Doctor Who and the Tardis. This song is a tale of a heartbroken traveller wandering through what appears to be a nameless wasteland, 'Wasted Years' is both thought-provoking and deep. Good stuff by main composer Smith.

Sea Of Madness ★ ★
Rhyming 'sadness' with 'madness' and containing a lyric mostly about those exact subjects, 'Sea Of Madness' appears to be one of the most profound songs Maiden have yet written.

Heaven Can Wait ★ ★ ★
"Is this in limbo or heaven or hell?" inquires Bruce through a sea of riffs and atmospherics, continuing the album's theme of confusion and spiritual removal. The film of the same name undoubtedly helped boost awareness of the song.

The Loneliness Of The Long Distance Runner ★ ★ ★
Evoking the miserablism of anyone running a long race when they don't have the motivation to win it, this song is an interesting subject for a metal band. But it works nonetheless.

Stranger In A Strange Land ★ ★ ★
Stranger in a Strange Land is the second single release from the Iron Maiden album. The lyrics are about the death of an Arctic Explorer and were once again written by Adam Smith. The song failed to chart significantly. One of the better-known Maiden songs from the era, 'Stranger In A Strange Land' may or may not be inspired by the famous Robert Heinlein novel of the 1960s. In either case it's still a lengthy, atmospheric piece of composition.

Deja-Vu ★ ★
"Feel like I've been here before!" chants Dickinson through this slight, self-explanatory bit of filler.

Alexander The Great ★ ★ ★ ★
Reading like a simple history lesson but injecting enough metal humour into its subject for credibility, this study of the famous Macedonian king is an epic way to finish the album.

Conclusion
Somewhere In Time is firstly a massive album because of its incredible artwork, of course. Getting past the cover – which shows Eddie as a bizarre cyborg hybrid of Clint Eastwood and the Terminator, amid a futuristic urban cityscape reminiscent of Blade Runner (but with very British wit, such as a digital clock showing the time 11:58... two minutes to midnight, right?) – is an effort in itself. The music, though, is of course worth the effort, as is every album from this golden era of Maiden's career. Huge fantastical themes abound (and would reach their logical conclusion on their next album, as we know) as well as a crisp production and some experimental touches that work perfectly. Somewhere In Time is often overshadowed by the vast Seventh Son Of A Seventh Son, which is a shame.

Overall rating: ★ ★ ★ ★

WASTED YEARS
(Single, 1986)

Tracklisting: Wasted Years / Reach Out
A precursor to the much more exciting 'Stranger In A Strange Land' single, 'Wasted Years' was at least useful in that it showed off the spanking new production to the fans.

Overall rating: ★ ★

STRANGER IN A STRANGE LAND
(Single, 1986)

Tracklisting: Stranger In A Strange Land / That Girl / Juanita

Signing off the Somewhere In Time album with this excellent single, possibly named after the epic sci-fi novel of the same name, Maiden warbled off into semi-progressive territory, anchored by that spiralling chorus from Bruce. Although the song is pretty much composed of that chorus and not much else, that's no bad thing, necessarily.

Overall rating: ★ ★ ★

SEVENTH SON OF A SEVENTH SON
(Album, 1988)

Moonchild ★ ★ ★
Introducing the theme of the doomed central character, 'Moonchild' takes the form of a malevolent deity sentencing his spirit to a life which is, shall we say, challenging.

Infinite Dreams ★ ★ ★
A mellow tune for such an early point in this album, 'Infinite Dreams' showcased the progress of the central concept character out of his childhood and towards the big fat single of 'Can I Play With Madness'. A keyboard wash – one of many on this atmosphere-heavy album – is heard and the riffage never really takes off, which is understandable given the song which follows it.

Can I Play With Madness ★ ★ ★ ★ ★
Fans' jaws dropped when they first heard 'Can I Play With Madness'. Longstanding listeners were in awe of its simple,

two-part harmony chorus – as with so many Maiden songs, also the track title – and the crisp, galloping riff that sat at its core. The mid-section, too, was a Harris-penned classic, initiated by a time change that took most people by surprise. Surprisingly, from this era of intense shredding solos, the guitar leads are weak and understated, perhaps deliberately so to facilitate airplay on pop stations. A breakdown to the a-cappella chorus is a masterstroke, as is the sudden ending. On the other hand, 'Can I Play With Madness' was a very, very commercial tune, which took a lot of people by surprise. Some fans were even up in arms, claiming that the band had made a cynical attempt to storm mainstream radio – and if this was the case, it worked admirably. As with all fans who see 'their' band embraced by the masses, there was more than a little jealousy and resentment. All of which makes 'Can I Play With Madness' one of the most controversial, and enjoyable, songs Maiden have ever recorded.

The Evil That Men Do ★ ★
A logical successor to 'Can I Play With Madness', but not quite as alluring or simple as that song, 'The Evil That Men Do' nailed that not particularly catchy phrase to a song of more or less standard quality. A slightly darker, less accessible outing for the pipes of Dickinson and the riffs of Murray and Smith, the song relieved those Maiden fans who had feared that the band might be heading uncontrollably into commercial territory.

Seventh Son Of A Seventh Son ★ ★
Repeating the number seven ad infinitum, the message that this is a concept album and – hey! – Maiden's seventh studio LP, the album's title track is not for the faint-hearted.

The Prophecy ★ ★
A frankly depressing moment in which the key character realises how pointless everything is ("and now it's too late..."), the song is almost the end of the line for Seventh Son.

The Clairvoyant ★ ★

"There's a time to live and a time to die", quoth the clairvoyant on this penultimate track. A good song it may be, but the album isn't going to end well...

Only The Good Die Young ★ ★ ★

It's goodbye to our central character and a portentous exposition of the nature of religion, as 'Only The Good Die Young' winds Seventh Son down with neither a bang nor a whimper, but a wail of guitars and vocal cords.

Conclusion

What an album, despite its ostentatious nature. Seventh Son Of A Seventh Son remains to this day the point at which many fans departed their favourite band, as the next LP was quite a change of atmosphere. The 1980s, then, were Maiden's decade. Remember them with this fantastic album.

Overall rating: ★ ★ ★ ★

CAN I PLAY WITH MADNESS
(Single, 1988)

Tracklisting: Can I Play With Madness / Black Bart Blues / Massacre

Once again Maiden and their handlers picked the obviously killer single from the new album. 'Can I Play With Madness' scored a high chart entry thanks to the impending Donington headline slot in 1988 – famously, at one point the loudest gig in history – and its utterly infectious chorus. Perhaps the sound was a little lightweight for some, but there was no arguing with its accessible, unforgettable quality. It remains the definitive stadium-era Maiden single.

Overall rating: ★ ★ ★ ★

THE EVIL THAT MEN DO
(Single, 1988)

Tracklisting: The Evil That Men Do / Prowler '88

Whether 'The Evil That Men Do' really needed to be released as a single at all – the job of promoting the Seventh Son Of A Seventh Son album had been done pretty efficiently by the Donington slot and the 'Can I Play With Madness' single, after all – is a moot point. Still, it was duly issued and like its predecessor did very well, even if it wasn't up to the previous single's standards. As for 'Prowler '88', there really wasn't much point at all.

Overall rating: ★ ★ ★

THE CLAIRVOYANT
(Single, 1988)

Tracklisting: The Clairvoyant / The Prisoner (Live) / Heaven Can Wait (Live)

The album had done well, judging by the number of singles Iron Maiden and their team released from it – and of the four issued, this was the weakest and least essential. Still, it was handy for those extra live tracks in the pre-filesharing age.

Overall rating: ★ ★

INFINITE DREAMS (LIVE)
(Single, 1989)

Tracklisting: Infinite Dreams (Live) / Killers (Live) / Still Life (Live)

A live single was by now becoming de rigueur for the modern, arena-straddling Maiden, and if any song was to be chosen from Seventh Son Of A Seventh Son, this might as well have been it. A slower, mellower tune than the previous singles, 'Infinite Dreams' didn't quite entrance the listener as much as anything else from the album, but it did at least showcase the fact that Maiden had a competent grasp on their more contemplative side.

Overall rating: ★ ★

NO PRAYER FOR THE DYING
(Album, 1990)

No Prayer for the Dying is the eighth studio album by the British heavy metal band Iron Maiden. The album marks the band's first line-up change since 1983, guitarist Adrian Smith left the band during the pre-production phase, unhappy with the musical direction the band was taking. Smith does have one co-writing credit on this album, for "Hooks in You." Smith was replaced by Janick Gers, who had previously worked on singer Bruce Dickinson's first solo-album, Tattooed Millionaire, and had previously worked with Fish and Ian Gillan. It was also to be Dickinson's last album with Iron Maiden for 9 years as he would leave the band to pursue a solo career. The album departed from the synth sound of the 80s albums to promote a more stripped back and straight forward rock music style. It also featured Iron Maiden's only number one single of their career: Bring Your Daughter... to the Slaughter.

Tailgunner ★ ★
Something of a treatise on the Dresden bombings of World War Two, 'Tailgunner' is more Biggles-style boy's own stuff from Bruce – but this time with some genuine pathos on the subject.

Holy Smoke ★ ★ ★
An excellent mickey-take out of religious televangelists, 'Holy Smoke' takes an unusual stance of arch mockery and even a glee at the downfall of the fools who were condemning The Number Of The Beast a few years before.

No Prayer For The Dying ★ ★
Ironically rather like a prayer itself, 'No Prayer…' is a dark, rather sad song that sees the narrator seated at a window and begging for help from above. Dark stuff.

Public Enema Number One ★ ★
Usually discounted because of its stupid title (comedy songs on B-sides, good; comedy songs on albums, bad. Bad, Steve, bad!), 'Public Enema Number One' (you can just imagine the geezerish chuckles in the rehearsal room when they thought that one up, as well as the rationales of "Well, we gotta show people we got a sense of humour, innit?") isn't as bad as the name suggests. But it is ultimately skippable.

Fates Warning ★ ★ ★
"The worst is yet to come, a hell for mankind" is the cheery conclusion of this depressing exposition on the state of the world and the fate of man.

The Assassin ★ ★ ★
Another contract-killer fantasy designed to spook anyone under 13, 'The Assassin' is a neatly-gauged run-through of nightmare violence.

Run Silent Run Deep ★ ★
Submarines, torpedoes ("the deadly fish will fly"), merchantmen – you have to love the detail Iron Maiden put into their war songs. One of the better songs of its type.

Hooks In You ★

A song that seems to be about our old friend Charlotte The Harlot from the mention of 'number 22', 'Hooks In You' is a slightly grisly warning about being hung up to die...

Bring Your Daughter... To The Slaughter ★ ★ ★

Arguably the most famous Iron Maiden song of all time 'Bring Your Daughter... to the Slaughter' was the band's first and only UK number one single. It was originally recorded and released by Bruce Dickinson on the soundtrack album to the movie A Nightmare on Elm Street 5: The Dream Child. Dickinson once explained what the song meant and how it related to the Nightmare on Elm Street films: "Here I tried to sum up what I thought Nightmare On Elm Street movies are really about, and it's all about adolescent fear of period pains. That's what I think it is - deep down. When a young girl first gets her period she bleeds and it happens at night, and so she is afraid to go to sleep and it's a very terrifying time for her, sexually as well, and Nightmare On Elm Street targets that fear. The real slaughter in the Freddie movies is when she loses her virginity. That is the rather nasty thought behind it all, but that's what makes those kind of movies frightening." An unexpectedly big success on the back of this rather average album. Who would have expected a chart-topper, 15 years after the band's inception?

Mother Russia ★ ★ ★

Were Iron Maiden really writing about perestroika when they wrote 'Mother Russia'? It seems so, implausibly enough. What a mixed bag of songs, eh?

Conclusion

Fear Of The Dark marked a turning point for Iron Maiden. The rationale behind its darker, rawer, less processed sound is understanable: just as Metallica – their nearest equivalents in terms of commercial success in metal at this point – had done between their ...And Justice For All and Metallica albums, Maiden knew that a stripping-down was required if they were to avoid disappearing into prog-rock territory. Not that prog-rock is necessarily a bad thing all the time, but it would have meant a change in direction for the band which some fans, already disheartened by the pretentious crispness of Seventh Son, might have deemed a step too far.

And so the band, with the about-to-leave Bruce Dickinson slightly dragging his heels, created a much lower-key album, in terms of both songs and production. However, in doing so they fell between two stools – a not-quite return to old-school, Di'Anno-style pub rawness, and a not-quite advance into the new alt.rock sounds that were about to emerge from America. The result is a mixed bag and not one that is often quoted by Maiden fans as one of their best albums.

Overall rating: ★ ★ ★

HOLY SMOKE
(Single, 1990)

Tracklisting: Holy Smoke / All In Your Mind / Kill Me Ce Soir

Released a few years after the main televangelism scandals, 'Holy Smoke' nonetheless bore the air of currency when released as a single in 1990.

Overall rating: ★ ★

BRING YOUR DAUGHTER... TO THE SLAUGHTER
(Single, 1990, No. 1)

Tracklisting: Bring Your Daughter... To The Slaughter / I'm A Mover / Communication Breakdown

A wholly unexpected No. 1 single from Iron Maiden, 'Bring Your Daughter...' was easily the strongest song on No Prayer For The Dying, even if it's a long way from classic 80s singles such as 'Can I Play With Madness'.

Overall rating: ★ ★ ★

FEAR OF THE DARK
(Album, 1992)

Be Quick Or Be Dead ★ ★ ★
The target of 'Be Quick Or Be Dead' might have been televangelists, or it might have been corporate finance-mongers. Either way, they were in for the sharp end of Bruce's tongue...

From Here To Eternity ★ ★
A decidedly sexual tale of a woman who 'rides' a 'motorbike'... you get the picture. But what are the devil and Charlotte The Harlot doing in there too?

Afraid To Shoot Strangers ★ ★
"The desert sand mound a burial ground" is just one of the more impenetrable metaphors in this abstract song, possibly written vaguely to avoid identifying one particular party as its subject.

Fear Is The Key ★ ★ ★
"You're outnumbered by the bastards until the day you die!" concludes Bruce in this song of futility, lost love and stale passion. It's not cheerful stuff, this, is it?

Childhood's End ★ ★ ★
War and its miserable consequences have often been the subject of Iron Maiden songs, and this one is one of the most thoughtful, painting a picture of children as war's ultimate victims.

Wasting Love ★ ★ ★
The grim postulations of a man who doesn't believe in love make 'Wasting Love' one of the darkest songs on this relentlessly downbeat album – one of the songs which made it a little hard to take for the fanbase.

The Fugitive ★
Pretty much based on the story of the famous TV series and then film, 'The Fugitive' sets the events of the tale to music and nothing else.

Chains Of Misery ★ ★
Madness and madmen, prophecy and prophets… what more could Iron Maiden do to make this relentlessly depressing album any more downbeat?

The Apparition ★ ★
"Can the soul live on and travel through space and time?" asks Dickinson in this thoughtful song which takes the form of a dialogue between Bruce and another unidentified person.

Judas Be My Guide ★ ★
"Is that all there is? Can I go now?" are the grimmest questions in this most dismal of songs, which is less than inspiring even if the music itself is well executed.

Weekend Warrior ★ ★ ★
The sort of song which might have been more suited to one of the early, Paul Di'Anno-led albums because it asks questions about being a real person and not merely a fake, 'Weekend Warrior' asks questions about identity and falsehood.

Fear Of The Dark ★ ★ ★ ★
A philosophical song that discusses the titular fear with some convincing images, the album's title track is among the best on this less-than-enthralling album.

Conclusion

What to say about this inconsistent album? Over time the appeal of Fear Of The Dark has waned, inevitably, with its sleeve art – perhaps the first Maiden cover to be genuinely creepy, rather than pleasurably so – perhaps its most immediately memorable element.

Overall rating: ★

BE QUICK OR BE DEAD
(Single, 1992)

Tracklisting: Be Quick Or Be Dead / Nodding Donkey Blues / Space Station No. 5

Releasing the standard two singles and moving on to more lucrative pastures with live albums, Maiden picked out the obviously palatable 'Be Quick...'.

Overall rating: ★ ★

FROM HERE TO ETERNITY
(Single, 1992)

Tracklisting: From Here To Eternity / Roll Over Vic Vella

A lady riding a bike – not the standard rock-single theme in the era of grunge and alternative rock...

Overall rating: ★ ★

A REAL LIVE DEAD ONE
(Album, 1993)

Tracklisting: The Number Of The Beast / The Trooper / Prowler / Transylvania / Remember Tomorrow / Where Eagles Dare / Sanctuary / Running Free / Run To The Hills / 2 Minutes To Midnight / Iron Maiden / Hallowed Be Thy Name / Be Quick Or Be Dead / From Here To Eternity / Can I Play With Madness / Wasting Love / Tailgunner / The Evil That Men Can Do / Afraid To Shoot Strangers / Bring Your Daughter... To The Slaughter / Heaven Can Wait / The Clairvoyant / Fear Of The Dark

The second live collection of Maiden's career was reasonably timed, although some might argue that only eight years after Live After Death it was not required. However, in those intervening eight years Iron Maiden had covered more road and air miles than ten 'normal' heavy metal bands combined, lending the release much credibility. The contents were absolutely predictable but the recording technology had improved since 1985 and no-one complained about the tracklisting or the excellent sound.

Overall rating: ★ ★ ★

HALLOWED BE THY NAME (LIVE)
(Single, 1993)

Tracklisting: Hallowed Be Thy Name (Live) / Wrathchild (Live)

Promoting the live album with appropriately live singles, Maiden plucked two reasonably commercial songs out of the bag...

Overall rating: ★ ★

FEAR OF THE DARK (LIVE)
(Single, 1993)

Tracklisting: Fear Of The Dark (Live) / Hooks In You (Live)

... even if making one of them the title track of the recent studio album in a ploy to boost the record's sales was a little suspect.

Overall rating: ★ ★

LIVE AT DONINGTON
(Album, 1993)

Tracklisting: Be Quick Or Be Dead / The Number Of The Beast / Wrathchild / From Here To Eternity / Can I Play With Madness / Wasting Love / Tailgunner / The Evil That Men Do / Afraid To Shoot Strangers / Fear Of The Dark / Bring Your Daughter... To The Slaughter / The Clairvoyant / Heaven Can Wait / Run To The Hills / 2 Minutes To Midnight / Iron Maiden / Hallowed Be Thy Name / The Trooper / Sanctuary / Running Free

Although the dust had barely settled on the A Real Live Dead One albums by the time that Live At Donington was released, there was a legitimacy to the release that permitted it shelf space among many thousands of Maiden fans. After all, if any band could claim a kind of ownership with this most venerable of British rock festivals, it would either be Ozzy or Maiden, both of whom had rocked the festival to its core when they played there. The songs included on this album often overlapped with the previous live albums (and even with Live After Death, inevitably) but Harris et al. had thrown in a few new tunes to avoid the cries of 'rip-off'.

Overall rating: ★ ★ ★

THE X FACTOR
(Album, 1995)

Blaze Bayley came into Iron Maiden on this album in order to replace the loss of Dickinson which had been clear on the previous album. The band hoped that Bayley would replace the fans lost by Dickinson's absence, however this album like the one previous largely flopped. Supporting the album was the X Factour tour. Much like the tour for their following album, Virtual XI, it was cut short after Blaze suffered a violent allergic reaction to certain elements used on the stages where the band performed. Man on the Edge and Lord of the Flies were released as singles with some success.

Sign Of The Cross ★ ★ ★
A sinister tale of death and redemption at the hands of 11 holy men, 'Sign Of The Cross' seems to indicate Harris' interest in religion at this point in his life.

Lord Of The Flies ★ ★ ★
The song is based on the book and film of the same name. The single was only released outside of the UK. Additional tracks on the single include covers from UFO and The Who. Iron Maiden frequently performed this song live during their Dance of Death tour from 2003–2004, making it one of very few Bayley era songs to survive in concerts after his departure "We are lord of the flies" muses Blaze Bayley on this song, co-written by Steve and Janick. It's a pretty decent observation of good versus evil, too.

Man On The Edge ★ ★ ★
This time it was the Michael Douglas film Falling Down which inspired the band, "car as hot as an oven" and all.

Fortunes Of War ★★
The fears enunciated by a man whose return from warfare has left him incapable of dealing with society, Deer Hunter style.

Look For The Truth ★
With the 'blade of hatred slicing through', it's apparent that 'Look For The Truth' is the tale of a man taking his own life. More depressing subject matter, eh?

The Aftermath ★★★
The horrors of war appear again in this dark song – where soldiers are mown down in gunfire and poppies bloom..

Judgement Of Heaven ★★
Asking if we would change our lives for the better given the chance, this song is another reasonably thought-out bit of religious questioning. It's pretty deep stuff.

Blood On The World's Hands ★★
"Brutality and aggression / Tomorrow another lesson" pontificate the band in this slightly preachy examination of social ills such as violence.

The Edge Of Darkness ★★★
Many Maiden songs take their inspiration from literature and film, as we've seen – but this one takes the cake, lifting its sentiments directly from Apocalypse Now and the book that inspired it (and this song's title, evidently), Heart Of Darkness.

2 A.M. ★★★
The sad tale of a drudge who gets home from work in the late evening and then sits pondering his meaningless existence, '2 AM' is one of the darkest songs here. Were the band going through a collective bout of depression, one wonders?

The Unbeliever ★★
A final peek into the grim subconscious of the modern male,

or just another world-weary whinge? Whatever – when Steve talked about finally letting himself express his feelings, this looks like the vehicle for expression he was referring to.

Conclusion
Blaze Bayley's first album with Iron Maiden – which he had joined from Wolfsbane in a move reminiscent of a football transfer from the Third Division to the Premiership – was attended by much expectation. When the results turned out to be not half bad, the fans were relieved. This was regarded as a vindication of the new line-up by Maiden and their associates, quite rightly – but it slightly obscured the fact that the album didn't contain any stone-cold classics.

Overall rating: ★ ★

MAN ON THE EDGE
(Single, 1995)

Tracklisting: Man On The Edge

A Bayley showcase that left many fans unconvinced. Still, the show had to go on...

Overall rating: ★

LORD OF THE FLIES
(Single, 1995)

Tracklisting: Lord Of The Flies

One of the more memorable songs in Maiden's recent history – but would the fans take to its relentlessly miserable tone?

Overall rating: ★ ★

BEST OF THE BEAST
(Album, 1996)

Tracklisting: Virus / Sign Of The Cross / Afraid To Shoot Strangers / Man On The Edge / Be Quick Or Be Dead / Fear Of The Dark / Holy Smoke / Bring Your Daughter... To The Slaughter / Seventh Son Of A Seventh Son / Can I Play With Madness / The Evil That Men Do / The Clairvoyant / Heaven Can Wait / Wasted Years / 2 Minutes To Midnight / Running Free / Rime Of The Ancient Mariner / Aces High / Where Eagles Dare / The Trooper / The Number Of The Beast / Revelations / The Prisoner / Run To The Hills / Hallowed Be Thy Name / Wrathchild / Killers / Remember Tomorrow / Phantom Of The Opera / Sanctuary / Prowler / Invasion / Strange World / Iron Maiden

As best-of albums go, compiling an Iron Maiden collection must have been a doddle. Other than the non-chronological tracklisting – which pleased and annoyed fans equally, depending on their stance towards such things – Best Of The Beast (see how the Eddie branding had become a staple by this point, eh?) was a simple, by the numbers walk through the band's long career, 18 years long at this point. The opening track, 'Virus', wasn't particularly exciting, unfortunately.

Overall rating: ★ ★ ★

VIRUS
(Single, 1996)

Tracklisting: Virus / Sanctuary / Wrathchild / My Generation / Doctor Doctor

Not bad as mid-to-late career Iron Maiden singles go, 'Virus' was created specifically to promote the Best Of The Beast album and suffered the fate that most such songs must face, i.e. it was virtually ignored. With the internet age still some years away, however, its status as a genuine rarity remained in place for some time, irrespective of its quality as a song.

Overall rating: ★ ★

VIRTUAL XI
(Album, 1998)

It was the second and final Iron Maiden album recorded with vocalist Blaze Bayley. The album is slightly unusual in the Iron Maiden catalogue for its extensive keyboard use. For this album all the keyboard parts were performed by band founder/bassist Steve Harris whereas on previous albums the keyboard parts were handled by session musician Michael Kenney. The album also had a reduced song-writing input from Janick Gers compared to the previous Iron Maiden albums since he joined the band in 1990. Just like the tour of The X Factor album, the tour for this album was cut short when Bayley suffered from an allergic reaction caused by certain elements used on the stage. As of 2010 the album had only just managed to sell a million copies worldwide making the album the poorest selling of the band's whole career. Bayley would depart the group after this album to be replaced by the returning Bruce Dickinson.

Futureal ★ ★ ★
At last, a reasonably good Blaze Bayley song, on which the ex-Wolfsbane shouter introduced Harris' themes of society crumbling away amid the advance of the computer.

The Angel And The Gambler ★ ★
"Do you feel lucky?" sneers Blaze, but he's no Clint Eastwood this time – this song deals with the love of gambling and the roll of the dice. How very Motörhead.

Lightning Strikes Twice ★ ★ ★
An excellent evocation of a night-time storm, accompanied by appropriately atmospheric music, makes 'Lightning Strikes Twice' one of the better songs of the Blaze era.

The Clansman ★
"We'll never be taken alive!" shouts William Wallace, sorry Blaze Bayley, before shouting "Freedom!" a lot. OK, now this is just silly.

When Two Worlds Collide ★ ★ ★
"For the hundredth time I check the declination" is not a line that is much used in popular music. Kudos to Dave Murray for putting together this astronomically-themed curio.

The Educated Fool ★ ★ ★ ★
One of the more intelligent, questioning songs that Maiden had been releasing over the last few years, 'The Educated Fool' asks big questions and sounds good in the process.

Don't Look To The Eyes Of A Stranger ★ ★
Pure paranoia in verse – warning the listener never to stop being alert. But where did all this worry come from?

Como Estais Amigos ★ ★ ★ ★
The nearest the band got to pure, emotional poetry in the Blaze era and a fine way to end any album, let alone this one.

Conclusion
And so Blaze Bayley's tenure with Iron Maiden came to an end. He had done a more than adequate job during his time with the band, but had been faced with insurmountable reluctance

to accept him from the fans as well as the fact that his voice was inferior to that of his flamboyant predecessor. The album on which he made his exit, Virtual XI, was marked by poor judgement on his band's part. Why base an album's title on the themes of football and the internet when the fanbase might not necessarily adhere to either? As with so many albums that deal with contemporary technology (see AC/DC's Blow Up Your Video), the subject matter dates rapidly and with it anything that has been written about it. Now that I.T. is a part of most people's lives but we're still not living in a virtual world, the concept of virtuality seems a bit outmoded before it's even begun. And so this album…

Overall rating: ★ ★

THE ANGEL AND THE GAMBLER
(Single, 1998)

Tracklisting: The Angel And The Gambler

More useful rather than essential sounds from the Blaze line-up, on its way out.

Overall rating: ★ ★ ★

FUTUREAL
(Single, 1998)

Tracklisting: Futureal

One of the better songs from this era, 'Futureal' stands up as evidence that the Blaze era could and did work out well from time to time. It was Bayley's legacy.

Overall rating: ★ ★

BRAVE NEW WORLD
(Album, 2000)

Brave New World marked the return of long-time lead singer Bruce Dickinson (who left in 1993) and guitarist Adrian Smith (who left in 1990) to the band. It was also the band's first studio recording with three guitar players, as Janick Gers stayed with the band after Smith's return. The album art and title song are references to the novel of the same name written by Aldous Huxley. The upper half of the album art was done by Derek Riggs, and is the last new artwork done by Riggs to be used on an Iron Maiden release. The bottom half was done by digital artist Steve Stone. Similarly, the line 'Brave new world' is repeated in the pre-chorus in an earlier song by the band, "Stranger in a Strange Land", from Somewhere in Time. Vocalist Bruce Dickinson calls this his favourite album, replacing Piece of Mind. The album did quite well in the charts reaching number 7 in the UK album charts and going gold as well as reaching number 37 in the USA.

The Wicker Man ★ ★ ★
The Wicker Man is based on the classic film of the same name and was written by Dickinson, Harris and Smith in collaboration. It was the first song released from the Brave New World album. The song even received a Grammy nomination in 2001 for Best Metal Performance but lost to Elite by the band Deftones. If you're going to reference classic UK horror cinema, you might as well use the best...

Ghost Of The Navigator ★ ★ ★
A cross between 'Rime Of The Ancient Mariner' and a Nile-gods tune from the Powerslave era, 'Ghost Of The Navigator' is fantasy-horror epitomised.

Brave New World ★
Based on the famous novel of the same name by Aldous Huxley, it has been a staple of live tours in recent times. It was the first track written since the return of Dickinson and Smith and is today considered as one of the group's finest tracks of all time. But not really that brave, either in sentiment, verse or execution. Bruce's delivery did give the band new vigour and elegance, but in terms of songwriting quality not much had changed since the Bayley era.

Blood Brothers ★ ★
The usual anti-war diatribe, I'm afraid.

The Mercenary ★ ★
Like 'The Trooper' but about money instead of war, this song doesn't break any new ground

Dream Of Mirrors ★ ★ ★
This song is another examination of reality versus illusion and, were it not for the endlessly repeated choruses, might be quite profound.

The Fallen Angel ★ ★
Maiden doing Morbid Angel? Certainly the demonic lyrics seem to be edging that way.

The Nomad ★
With lines like "Nomad, you're the rider so mysterious" you know you don't need this song.

Out Of The Silent Planet ★ ★ ★
Not, apparently an homage to the C.S. Lewis novel of the same name, but a decent sci-fi workout nonetheless.

The Thin Line Between Love And Hate ★ ★
Perhaps the most philosophical song Maiden have written to date, this track ends the album perfectly.

Conclusion

Brave New World, announced by promo shots of the band waving flaming torches and hype that the new old line-up with Bruce on board would be the be-all and end-all of modern heavy metal, didn't quite match up to expectations. Y'know, all the elements were there – the three guitars (which on record sounded no heavier than two, strangely enough), the air-raid siren wails, the bass fills, the galloping drums – but Iron Maiden in the new millennium weren't really too convincing.

Overall rating: ★ ★

THE WICKER MAN
(Single, 2000)

Tracklisting: The Wicker Man / Man On The Edge (Live)

A great institution in film such as The Wicker Man would translate well to heavy metal, you might think, and so it does – largely. The B-side is more or less irrelevant in this download era.

Overall rating: ★ ★

OUT OF THE SILENT PLANET
(Single, 2000)

Tracklisting: Out Of The Silent Planet / Wasted Years (Live)

A good choice of single, 'Out Of The Silent Planet' worked on most levels even if it's no 'Run To The Hills'. The live B-side? Forget it.

Overall rating: ★ ★ ★

ROCK IN RIO
(Album, 2002)

Tracklisting: Intro / The Wicker Man / Ghost Of The Navigator / Brave New World / Wrathchild / 2 Minutes To Midnight / Blood Brothers / Sign Of The Cross / The Mercenary / The Trooper / Dream Of Mirrors / The Clansman / The Evil That Men Do / Fear Of The Dark / Iron Maiden / The Number Of The Beast / Hallowed Be Thy Name / Sanctuary / Run To The Hills

Live and best-of time again – either because six years between such events is deemed too long nowadays, or because Bruce's return to the band needed to be accompanied by more celebratory releases – and Maiden did their usual thing with aplomb, supplying a sweet set of classics with a few new songs involved. What was new this time around, and was made much of by the band and management, was the spiffing new digital sound that made everything much, much clearer than the live albums of yore. No wonder they accompanied the album with a DVD – a ruse which, it is said, every subsequent tour from now on will follow.

Overall rating: ★ ★ ★

EDWARD THE GREAT
(Album, 2002)

Tracklisting: Run To The Hills / The Number Of The Beast / Flight Of Icarus / The Trooper / 2 Minutes To Midnight / Wasted Years / Can I Play With Madness / The Evil That Men Do / The Clairvoyant / Infinite Dreams / Holy Smoke / Bring Your Daughter... To The Slaughter / Man

On The Edge / Futureal / The Wicker Man / Fear Of The Dark (Live)

Sequenced chronologically to avoid mass annoyance among the more anal of the Maiden fanbase, Edward The Great was an unremarkable best-of, taking in the singles and basically nothing else. That said, EMI and the band did take the time to produce a limited-edition box set, a luxurious metal case with shot glasses and other fluff in it, at a correspondingly luxurious asking price. Just as Best Of The Beast was for young metallers born in about 1980, Edward The Great was the perfect entrée into Maiden for your average baggy-arsed-jeans kid who arrived in the mid-80s.

Overall rating: ★ ★ ★

WILDEST DREAMS
(Single, 2003)

Tracklisting: Wildest Dreams / Pass The Jam / Blood Brothers (Orchestral Version)

Wait! Where's the melody? Where previous Iron Maiden singles had been selected for release because they jumped off a mountain and rollercoastered into new melodic territory, 'Wildest Dreams' simply added a chorus to a verse (in the same key!) and carried on without much variation until the end. As for 'Pass The Jam'… enough said.

Overall rating: ★

DANCE OF DEATH
(Album, 2003)

The first album to be released in Japan before the US and UK. The album was reasonably successful worldwide and marked the first entry into songwriting by drummer Nicko McBrain. The entire band actually contributed to the writing of songs on this album. The Dance of Death World Tour was the tour supporting the album. Dance of Death once again brought costumes to Maiden's stage show. During "Dance of Death," Bruce Dickinson would wear theatrical masks and a cape while moving around the stage; at the end he would dress as the Grim Reaper for the final chorus. During the song "Paschendale", Dickinson would sometimes wear a traditional British Infantryman suit as worn during World War I and act out his death onstage during the song.

Wildest Dreams ★
The fact that 'Wildest Dreams' was thought to be the most commercially sellable song on this album speaks volumes. With this song as evidence, you'd be forgiven for thinking that Iron Maiden (and in particular Steve Harris) had lost their touch for songwriting, even on a temporary basis. Not good at all…

Rainmaker ★ ★ ★
A semi-biblical, fully fantastical tale of a sojourn in the desert – visions, magical powers and all. This was Maiden's lyric machine fully back in action.

No More Lies ★ ★
With its meaning obscured, it falls to 'No More Lies' to stand up as a reminder of how accomplished Maiden could be as musicians. But that three-guitar attack should be much heavier, Kevin…

Montsegur ★ ★ ★
The blood-soaked tale of Montségur and the Knights Templar translates well into Maiden language, leading to an early high point.

Dance Of Death ★ ★
Dancing with the dead in a scene straight out of HP Lovecraft, Bruce does his best to make this sound scary. He fails.

Gates Of Tomorrow ★ ★
"You can't blame a madman if you go insane," chirps Dickinson meaninglessly, on a song which is far from Maiden's finest hour.

New Frontier ★
"The spawn of a man, the devil has planned?" Iron Maiden are winging it now, no matter what they say…

Paschendale ★ ★
Much, much better, as is usually the way when Maiden tackle a real-life war story. The tale of Paschendale stands up well on this frankly drab album.

Face In The Sand ★
Another 'life-is-terrible' meditation, and not really one that is required on this journey, thanks.

Age Of Innocence ★ ★ ★
"You can't protect yourselves even in your own home" say Maiden here, on a rare outing into the real world. Does it work? Lyrically, no; musically, reasonably well.

Journeyman ★ ★ ★
A welcome entry into acoustic territory (which Maiden should do more often) provides an unusual and welcome end to Dance Of Death.

Conclusion

With its digital artwork and unprepossessing lead-off single, 'Wildest Dreams', Dance Of Death (now there's an album title stolen from mid-80s Marillion if ever I saw one) didn't stand much chance. Like Brave New World and, well, every Iron Maiden album going as far back as Seventh Son Of A Seventh Son, the record was OK but not great. It was time, people were concluding in their thousands, to admit that where Iron Maiden now belonged was on the stage rather than in the studio.

Overall rating: ★ ★

RAINMAKER
(Single, 2003)

Tracklisting: Rainmaker / Dance Of Death (Orchestral Version) / More Tea Vicar

A useful entrée to the Dance... phenomenon with highly disposable bonus tracks.

Overall rating: ★ ★

NO MORE LIES
(Single, 2004)

Tracklisting: No More Lies / Paschendale (Orchestral Version) / Journeyman (Electric Version)

A second single from this unprepossessing album was hardly needed, but the electric 'Journeyman' was interesting at least.

Overall rating: ★ ★

A MATTER OF LIFE AND DEATH
(Album, 2006)

A Matter of Life and Death is the fourteenth studio album by English heavy metal band Iron Maiden. It was released on 25 August 2006 in Italy and Finland, 28 August worldwide, and 5 September 2006 in the United States, Canada and Japan. It is the first album in Iron Maiden's career to enter the U.S. Billboard charts in the top 10 and the third album where Steve Harris has had a song writing credit on every track, and has seen significant chart success in many other countries. The album was met with positive reviews. Metal Hammer rated the album 10/10 and stated that "Iron Maiden have utterly surpassed themselves", Kerrang! Rated it 5/5 and said "Another Iron Maiden classic... Keeps what long-time fans loved about the band alive." Classic Rock also awarded it Album of the Year, and the band won an award, voted by Classic Rock readers, for the album. Rolling Stone gave the album 3 stars out of 5, finding the music and lyrics "relevant." However, the magazine also claims that "the songs now march where they once galloped", implying that the band is "aging gracefully".

Different World ★ ★
The second single released from the album. The song has often been compared as a tribute to Thin Lizzy due to the low sounding melodies which sound similar to those of Phil Lynot. Iron Maiden albums usually have reasonably good first tracks, and this is no exception: worth your time and then a bit more. The song is featured in the skateboarding video game Tony Hawk's Downhill Jam. The song peaked at number 3 in the UK charts and reached number 8 in the US charts.

These Colours Don't Run ★ ★ ★
Despite the great title, this is no aggro song – it's a call for peace, effectively, and all the better for it.

Brighter Than A Thousand Suns ★ ★ ★
Lyrically profound at last and musically memorable, this song fits in most of Maiden's considerable ambitions and does it well.

Pilgrim ★ ★ ★
With a slow riff breakdown to die for and understated riffage, 'Pilgrim' is a filler tune that thinks it's a single.

Longest Day ★ ★ ★
Valhalla? Valkyries? A high body count? What's not to like, lyrically or musically?

Out Of The Shadows ★ ★ ★
With enigmatic imagery dotted through every verse, this song may not say much but it sounds intriguing.

The Reincarnation Of Benjamin Breeg ★ ★
The debut single from the 2006 album, The Reincarnation of Benjamin Breeg was released in August of 2006. On 17 July 2006, a music video for the song was uploaded on the band's official website. It had initially been released only for paying fan club members, but it was leaked within minutes and viewed by many fans who posted the link on various Iron Maiden discussion forums. The video displays them performing in the studio along with classic photos and clips of the band over their lengthy career. A useful lead-off single to create interest in the album, '…Breeg' even had its own website for a while. The song isn't actually that great, but that wasn't the point.

For The Greater Good Of God ★ ★ ★
Does Harris' religious questioning never end? Apparently not, fortunately for us when it results in songs like this.

Lord Of Light ★ ★
A peace song, a Satan song, a philosophy song – does it matter as long as it's a good song?

The Legacy ★ ★ ★ ★
A truly vast epic to wind things down? A standard Maiden trick – but this is a special one...

Conclusion
Where A Matter Of Life And Death recoups ground lost over the previous decade by a series of unremarkable albums is not in the extraordinary quality of its songs, not by any means: the songs are merely good, for the most part. What does make the album stand out is that Harris, who wrote most of the songs on the album as always, allows himself to stretch out into the epic, progressive territory that he has always enjoyed – but from which he has always restrained himself from full entry in case the band diverges too far from its original course. Not that A Matter Of Life And Death is a Yes or ELP album, however – but there is definitely a sense of experimentation and an unhurried approach to the songs which suits the zeitgeist perfectly. We now live in a culture where heavy, complex and/or challenging music is treated with much more affection and tolerance than beforehand, when the three-minute pop single was king for everyone (not just for under-20s, as it is today) – and in such a relatively mature environment, master songwriters like Harris, especially with such a lengthy career behind him, can thrive. The verdict? Not that this album is Maiden's best, or even their second or third or fifth best. But it's been received with an enthusiasm sorely lacking in the appreciation afforded the last few albums, and that, friends, can only be a good thing.

Overall rating: ★ ★ ★

THE FINAL FRONTIER
(Album, 2010)

Tracklisting: Satellite 15... The Final Frontier / El Dorado / Mother of Mercy / Coming Home / The Alchemist / Isle of Avalon / Starblind / The Talisman / The Man Who Would Be King / When The Wild Wind Blows.

The Final Frontier is going to be Iron Maiden's amazing 15th studio album. At 76 minutes and 34 seconds, it is the band's longest studio album to date. It will be their first album since the release of A Matter of Life and Death in 2006, the longest gap to date between two consecutive Iron Maiden studio albums. Melvyn Grant, a long-time contributor to the band's artwork, created the cover art for the album.

One single has already been released from the album called El Dorado, it was made available on the band's website as a free digital download.

Critics are largely divided on the album, saying that it will likely be the group's last ever album and that the name is possibly an indication of the beginning of the end. Most critics say that it will be an album that stays true to the genuine and loyal Iron Maiden fans.

ABOUT CODA BOOKS

Most Coda books are edited and endorsed by Emmy Award winning filmmaker and concert promoter Bob Carruthers. Over the last 20 years Bob has filmed and promoted tours, concerts and made documentaries all over Britain and Europe in venues ranging from Hammersmith Odeon to Murrayfield Stadium, with artists such as Bryan Adams, Spandau Ballet, Jethro Tull, Status Quo and Katherine Jenkins.

The 'Uncensored On the Record' series explores the careers of many of music's greatest legends, encompassing a wide range of genres including classic rock, pop, heavy metal, punk, country, classical and soul.

For more information visit **www.codabooks.com**.

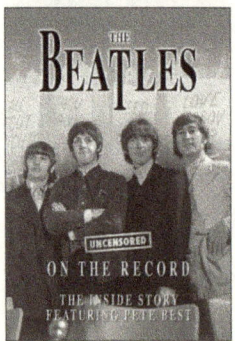

www.ingramcontent.com/pod-product-compliance
Lightning Source LLC
LaVergne TN
LVHW041545070426
835507LV00011B/936